# In Search

# Of

# Meaning

# In Search of Meaning

*My Struggles for Identity and Self-discovery*

## Sabir Abdur Rahman

*MV Publishers*

Published by MV Publishers, a subsidiary of Muslim Voice, 12719 Hillmeade Station Dr, Bowie, MD 20720, USA.
MVPublishers@muslimvoice.org

ISBN 978-1-956601-10-7

First edition 2023

United States of America

Sabir Abdur Rahman, 1940 –

In Search of Meaning

ISBN 978-1-956601-10-7

*For*

*My two grand fathers*

*Maulvi Muhammad Ismail and Choudhary Jamal Din*

*and my parents*

*Choudhary Ali Muhammad and Khadija Begum*

# Contents

☐

# *Foreword*

Over sixty years ago, Viktor Emil Frankl described the search for life's meaning as the central human motivational force and founded a new school of psychotherapy, Logotherapy, within the existential and humanistic psychology theories. His autobiography "Man's Search for Meaning" published in 1959 and based on his experiences as a Holocaust survivor became an international best-selling book. Frankl's central idea is that one must find meaning in one's life through work and suffering which would lead to fulfillment and happiness. In reading Sabir Rahman's "In Search of Meaning," I can detect an underlying echo of Frankl's theme, the Will to Meaning, the desire to find a meaning in life and free will.

Sabir has seen much change in his social and cultural environment over his lifetime. Early in his childhood he went through the trauma of forced migration, comparable to the Holocaust by some, when in 1947 the British India was divided into two countries. He still lives through the pain and anguish of that uprooting experience. Then, at an early age he migrated to America, driven not by force this time, but by force of circumstance. Each time moving from one world to another, his soul was torn apart by the pulls exerted by the values and norms of a different culture and society. Thus, this book is a story of his struggles for his identity and self-discovery.

Sabir's search for meaning is also driven by the stark contrast between the culture of his upbringing and that which surrounded him through his adult life. One was deeply religious, traditional, authoritative, and culturally homogenous; the other is modern with its secular, rational and science centered, multicultural and pluralistic. How has he been able to bridge the chasm? I'd say remarkable well.

Many of us struggle with the challenges thrown up by modernity and science to our religious beliefs. The author shows how to find a reconciliation between the two by resorting to our individual free will rather than looking for solutions in the teachings of organized religion. There is an enormous scope in applying reason and logical analysis to some of the thorniest conundrums faced by all religions. This approach which goes back to the rationalist scholars of the Islamic Golden Age (Mutazilites), is much needed in the world of today which confronts enormous challenges in the face of scientific and technological development eroding the core of religious beliefs and ethical moorings. Ever since Nietzsche declared God to be dead, men of faith have strived for religious revival. This book is an attempt to fill that 'God-shaped-hole' left in its wake. In his discourse, people of all faiths should find a rational approach to the solution of not only the philosophical issues but also to the day-to-day questions of practices, ethics and norms so often confounded by the conflicting interpretations by the stalwarts of the organized religion.

The author is uniquely qualified to address the questions faced by many in this age of social change. He has an excellent command over the scriptures of not only the three Abrahamic religions, but of Hinduism as well. His activism in various Muslim community organizations and inter-faith forums has provided him with a panoramic view of all faith systems. He has been an invited speaker and discussant on numerous such platforms where many of the ideas included in the book originated.

I have been privileged to hold in-depth discussions with Sabir over many years of our long association and friendship. I have found him to be exceptionally receptive to new ideas and rational arguments. I have learned a lot through such exchanges, and hope that the readers of this book will too.

Jamshed Y. Uppal, Ph.D.
Associate Professor
Catholic University of America, Washington, DC
June 4, 2023

# *Preface*

Confucius is reported to have said that 'there is nothing more real than what cannot be seen and there is nothing more certain than what cannot be heard.' That would appear to be the essence of Faith. In an uncertain world surrounded by dangers and fears of all kinds, humans have always sought solace in some unseen and unknowable power that may be watching over them and protecting them. In Hebrews 11:1, we find St. Paul telling us that 'faith is the assurance of things hoped for, the conviction of things not seen.' Thus, faith fills the void created by apprehensive uncertainty. It may calm the anxiety of the fear of all the dangers which constantly lurk all around. This strong need for faith also provides an opportunity for exploitation by those who desire to exercise power over others. The original founders of faith seldom insisted on total obedience to any particular definitions or methods. But those who followed later to assume the leadership of the faith, began to define it in ways which the founder may never have intended. These later self-appointed guardians of faith instituted the rules which they demanded to be followed on penalty of punishment.

Faith is based on belief in, and acceptance of, a superhuman entity, a supreme power which is held to be the source of all creation and watcher and protector over it. But humanity does not find agreement as to how to define that entity, that superpower. Humanity does not even agree on a single set of commands which are supposed to have been given by that power to regulate human life. That gives rise to multiple claims of faithfulness, each proclaiming to be the only true faith. And each faith claims a founder for that faith who is held to be the source of all teachings. These founders – Moses, Jesus, Muhammad, Buddha – may have been driven by a desire to reform and improve their society and may have faced immense opposition from the powers in control of their societies during their time. But they succeeded in getting their reform message across to at least a segment of their society. That segment grew over time to become a forceful power which may have established a

1

ruling control over large territories and peoples. Those who took over the leadership of these people – spiritual and temporal – proceeded to define and redefine those principles to regulate their society; mostly to control their people. These principles would become a source of power for those in control, and therefore they would find it necessary to differentiate their definitions from those of other established faiths, with whom they would find themselves in conflict.

Faith is one source of differentiation and conflict. There are others. National identity and cultural and socio-economic systems also lead to differentiation and conflict. These conflicts may remain passive until one system or another gains military superiority. Then the conflicts become dangerous and destructive, because human nature demands and insists that the advantage should be employed to overpower and subjugate.

Some religious theologians, some scholars and philosophers have attempted to define the ideal human behavior which could lead to a blissful orderly peace on earth with justice for all. Being gifted writers, they have written their ideas into beautifully composed prose. Those who read these writings admire them and praise them abundantly. But the abundant admiration and praise have always failed to persuade humanity to actually follow the advice contained in those beautiful pieces of prose. Humanity seldom adopts them or acts on those ideal principles which are designed to lead humanity to peace with justice. There has never been a time in the recorded life of humanity when peace and justice prevailed in the world.

Words like justice and peace are complicated. They mean different things to different people. Sometimes they mean different things to the same people under different circumstances. What we consider to be justice in making amends for things done to us by others, is not considered by us to be justice when others react to correct the same things done by us to them. When we are in bondage to someone else who would force us to submit to their oppression, we protest it as injustice. When we use our power to subjugate others, we then demand that no one should protest against us. Any who points to our aggression would be demonized by us and by our friends and accomplices in the enterprise. But we consider it our God given right to scream aggression when someone else rises to fight, even when they are fighting to defend themselves against our aggression. If we have the power and the might to drive our point of view through, then whatever we do is right; it is justice. So, justice is, as Glaucon told Socrates, 'The advantage of the stronger'. Even though Jesus has told us 'not to judge', we proceed to judge and deliver our verdict against any who do not join us. Because any who are not with us, are against us, and must be treated as enemies. We are proud of our faith, our culture and our socio-economic system. We treat our faith, our values and our systems to be superior to all others. That sense of superiority endows us with self-righteousness, which leads us to harshly judge the people with whom we disagree and proceed to condemn and dismiss them.

Since early in my life, I have been troubled by one question; what is the purpose of life? I have thought long and hard but have not been able to find a satisfactory answer. I have talked to a large number of people, but no one has been able to guide me to an acceptable answer. In fact, I have discovered that, perhaps, nobody has even asked, considered or pondered this question. Attempts at answers in religious terms such as what God wants from humans or the human obligation to God, or in personal terms as life being pursuit of happiness, do not seem to satisfy me. Although I have not been able to find a satisfactory clue to the purpose of life, my curiosity led me to other questions about faith and human behavior. And I found those areas also very puzzling. If all faiths are built on belief in God, then why are there so many of them, all antagonistic to each other? The followers of three Abrahamic faiths pledge allegiance to Abraham. Then how did they become three different faiths, hostile to each other? If God is the creator of humanity and therefore God of all humans, then how can protagonists of each faith claim Him exclusively for themselves? Does God take sides for one segment of His creation against another segment? It is not possible. It is not reasonable. The never-ending conflict between different groups of humans cannot be condoned by God.

Troubled by such questions I began to study scriptures and religious writings. I found some wonderful parts in all scriptures and also some difficult passages. According to Karen Armstrong, St. Augustine advocated to interpret difficult passages to give them positive interpretation. That is good advice. I did not find it difficult to follow.

But I did find the attitude of the self-appointed guardians of religions very difficult to accept. The great reformers who dedicated their lives to improving the quality of human life, had instituted and taught excellent principles, designed not only to help humanity but also to unite it with harmony. Then came these self-appointed leaders of faith who redefined the excellent teachings of the great reformers into a set of rules designed to turn the faith into an organized religion, with them planted in the seat of power. They appointed themselves as the ultimate religious authority and demanded total obedience from all believers of their faith. They enforced their demands by frightening everyone with the horrible punishment of burning in hell. These religious leaders made league with temporal authority, and they together continued to control the destiny of the masses while giving their own selves the pass.

No human has ever been asked if they wanted this life and wanted to be born into it. Born without consultation or consent, into a life not of their own making, forced to live it by rules they did not participate in making but were just imposed on them, they found themselves helpless and unable to disobey the temporal commands of the rulers and the theocratic commands of the self-appointed religious authority. Civilization is supposed be an advanced stage of human social and cultural development. We are supposed be civilized by now, but we continue to allow ourselves to be controlled by those who grab power and assume authority over us. It must begin to change.

But it seems to be next to impossible to make a significant impact on the thought process which has been off the proper path for a long time and continues to veer further off course. Everyone is so comfortable with the status quo and so committed to follow the established norm that no matter how much evidence is presented to them about the established system being seriously at variance with what their cherished Scriptures actually teach, they just will not pay heed. This situation is so beyond reason, that change for the better appears be impossible, making the reformer helpless. They have eyes, but cannot see. Or refuse to see.

Yet, I keep on hoping and wishing and dreaming. This is my attempt at redefining the parameters of faith that ought to transition the practice of faith from the control of the self-appointed religious authority to individual choice, that would transform faith from dogma to reason, and hopefully free many of us from the inhibitions imposed on us by the fear inspired by the religious authority with constant reminder of hell. I believe in God, but I am convinced that God has given us free will and has left us alone to exercise that free will. He does not control our life nor interfere with it on an ongoing basis. With that conviction, which I acquired over a long-drawn struggle to overcome the indoctrination which I received when I was growing up and well beyond, I have been writing these articles and sharing them with some of my friends and relatives, especially my brother Dr. Abdur Rahim Choudhary and my long-time friend Dr. Jamshed Uppal. Finally, Abdur Rahim decided to create a collection of many of these articles to publish them as a book. He is good at such things. He has created an online platform as Muslim Planet and has established a publishing organization as Muslim Voice. His writing ability is much superior to mine. He has edited my articles and vastly improved the message and the narrative. It goes without saying that I am grateful. He is my younger brother. The love and care for each other which our parents taught us, make it unnecessary to use words to thank each other. Sentiments are very clear and loud.

Jamshed made a huge contribution by further editing and enhancing the manuscript and by writing a Foreword.

I am eternally grateful to Abdur Rahim and Jamshed. Without their help and enormous contribution, this project would not have been possible.

Sabir Abdur Rahman
June 4, 2023

# 1.  *Finding Faith in God*

*A rational analysis allows a path that acknowledges allegiance to God, yet without allegiance to an organized religion —that seeks the spiritual side of God without the legalistic and often judgmental side of a religion. This ascribes to God a role that lays down the laws of causality operating on a universal scale.*

Humans have a strong need to believe in something. Many believe in God. Some, who may claim not to believe in God, still would believe in something, even if that something is a symbol or an idea. Some believe in the flag of their country, some believe in the constitutional legal system, and some believe in the party or the group they belong to. But everyone believes in something, because to believe in something is the primal human need.

Those who believe in God constitute the largest segment of humanity, by far the majority of all humans. But they do not all agree on how to believe in God. Each group claims to believe in God and follow the message from God received through a chosen Divine Messenger, but each group insists that the message it follows is unique and is the only true message. Each group also claims that only their method of believing in God is correct.

Humans have believed in God as far back as the history goes. They have also felt a strong need to be able to personally relate to God. While they always believed in the supreme entity that is all powerful, all knowing and all seeing, in possession of the infinite and ultimate creative powers, they always made physical representations of God to satisfy their primal need to see and touch God. Since different people made different representations and images, the idea developed of polytheistic religions. While insiders may believe only in that supreme entity as the One True God, with many different representations and manifestations of that Supreme Authority to satisfy their need to see and touch God, to the outsiders it may have appeared as if they believed in and worshipped many different Gods.

Therefore, the outsiders referred to them as polytheists, and even differentiated between One God by writing the name in English with capital G, and many gods by writing the name with small g.

Abraham may have introduced the concept of monotheism and the idea of the unseen God. These ideas took a long time to be understood and be defined. Moses finally formulated the idea into a concrete definition by insisting that all his followers be strictly monotheistic and should believe in the One Supreme God who was so transcendental that it was impossible for humans to comprehend Him. Moses also taught his congregation that God is so far beyond the reach and comprehension of the humans that He wants his creatures to simply accept Him as such and follow His guiding message that was delivered through Moses and would be redelivered, with or without modifications, through the future Prophets.

Moses impressed upon his congregation that God demanded that they should not make His graven images.

The Human need to see and touch God is so strong that the Israelites did not take long to make a golden calf as their representation of the Lord, God of Israel. Moses destroyed it and kept his congregation in check as long as he was alive. But for almost a millennium, the Israelites kept on shifting between worshipping God through various kinds of images, and worshipping God without such images. The iconoclastic monotheism was not fully adopted by the Israelites until sometime after their return from Babylon.

Until then, they were still making graven images. They were not the only ones who made and worshipped images, just about everyone in their region were doing it. Even after the Israelites stopped making such images, many others continued to worship images for whom they had built houses of worship with images presiding over those houses. Then the Greeks and Romans came with their own gods, and they caused the images of those gods to be placed in the temple of Israel. Greeks, at one time, even tried to force the Jews to give up their Jewish religion, adopt the Greek religion and worship Greek gods.

Jews were able to survive the Greek attempt at their forced conversion. Romans did not try to force their religion on the Jews, but the Romans did hold the Roman religion to be superior.

Claims of superiority of faith are a manifestation of Power. Those who hold Power and control the destiny of others, are able to lay a claim to the superiority of what they believe and are able to make that claim stick. When Greeks and then Romans were controlling the destiny of a large part of humanity, they could proudly hold their faith, whatever it was, to be superior to all others. And they did.

Christianity began in the iconoclastic tradition of Judaism because its founding preacher was himself a Jew. But the followers of Jesus, who believed that he was born by a Divine Miracle to a Virgin Mother, began to debate the nature of Jesus about 250 years after the birth of Christianity. The debate centered on the question; is Jesus of the Virgin Birth created or uncreated? That debate raged for close to a century and the majority of the faithful arrived at Trinity. Although opposition to that idea of Trinity remained active for about 500 years, Trinity ultimately became the foundation of the faith and has remained so ever since. As a result, the image of Jesus has become a permanent feature of every church and many Christian homes. Father, Son and Holy Spirit are distinct and separate from each other, but each is God.

In a philosophical understanding of Trinity, there is only One God, and there are three different manifestations of the same One God.

Hindus believe in one Supreme God whom they call Ishwar. They worship his many different manifestations, whose images are placed in Hindu Temples and also in people's homes. But they never make an image of Ishwar. The three most common manifestations are Brahma, Vishnu and Shiva, who form the Divine Trilogy. But there are many more, both male and female, whose images are placed and worshipped all over India and wherever in the world the Hindus live.

While Hindus would hold that they are worshipping One True God through the images of these various manifestations, to the outsiders it would seem that they are worshipping many gods and the outsiders would consider the Hindus to be polytheists.

Many years back the Inter Faith Council of Metro Washington (IFC) decided to write a book for use in high schools. It asked its faith members to each write a chapter to describe their faith. The Hindu Chapter was written by D. C. Rao. When he finished the draft and circulated among selected members of IFC, he asked a question at the end. He mentioned that there was a lot of talk about monotheism, but the discussion of that idea was limited to Islam, Christianity and Judaism. He asked; "Don't you know that Hinduism is a monotheistic faith?" The question is valid and the answer, to be accurate, would likely be in the positive. The monotheism of Hindus is represented by their belief in Ishwar whom they hold as the transcendental One True God. Ishwar is held to be the Unseen God whose images are never made. But it is unclear if more than a handful of people outside of Hinduism, and even many within Hinduism, would acknowledge this.

A new faith was born in Punjab, India, in the 16th century. It was founded by Guru Nanak (1469-1539) who preached monotheism. His followers are called Sikh, who are monotheists and believe in One God. But the personality of the founding teacher has been elevated by the believers to such transcendental heights that it has become just about impossible to differentiate between Nanak and God. Nanak is Guru and God is Waheguru.

Similar to Jesus in Christianity, pictures of Nanak grace all Sikh houses of worship (called Gurudwara, meaning the gateway to the Guru) and many Sikh homes.

Islam has maintained the iconoclastic monotheism taught by Moses. Muslims are fiercely monotheistic and iconoclastic, and they jealously guard the oneness of God, for which they use the Arabic word *Tawheed* (meaning oneness or unity). Literally *Tawheed* means "unification" (making something one) or "asserting oneness", and it comes from the Arabic verb *wahhada* which itself means to unite, unify or consolidate. Muslims follow the Divine Message received from the One True Unseen God through his final Prophet Muhammad.

Muslims respect and revere Muhammad to a very high degree but do not worship him and are fiercely opposed to making any images of him.

Human longing for imagery is so strong, that one would be able to find exceptions to this fierce opposition of Muslims to making images of Muhammad; such images are available in some parts of the world and people are known to possess such images.

However, Muslim consider Muhammad to be human just like any other human but elevated above all other humans because he was chosen by God to deliver and explain the Divine Message.

Being totally opposed to any kind of representation of God or any concept of God that even remotely suggests a departure from the strict Unity and Oneness of God, Muslims look with great disdain at any attempt or action that appears to imply even a slight departure from that absolute

Oneness. For example, many Muslims would condemn worship of the Hindu images and would consider them polytheists. Muslims, likewise, reject Trinity as a departure from an absolute unity of God, and some of them might consider Christians as polytheists or at least Trinitarians or tritheist.

Muslims maintain that the Divine Message continued after Moses and was delivered by Jesus and finally by Muhammad. They equally revere Moses, Jesus and Muhammad. Further, some of them would fault Jews and Christians for not accepting the final Divine Message and the final Messenger, just as some Christians would fault Jews for not accepting Christ.

There are other religions such as Baha'i, Buddhism, Confucianism, Jainism, Shinto, Taoism, and Zoroastrianism, and possibly others. They all believe in God in their own way.

All religions not only disagree externally with each other in how they look at God, they often are not united internally either. Each faith group consists of subgroups which may not always agree with each other. Sometimes their internal differences may become just as contentious, or maybe even more so, than their differences with other faiths. And they all become so insistent on their own exclusive and unique righteousness, and their strong condemnation of everyone else, that it becomes divisive and hostile.

If one carefully studies the Divine Message of each variation, one finds that the messages in all traditions essentially teach the same things. And it is just the opposite of divisiveness and hostility; it is a message that teaches us to respect the other and get along with each other through cooperation.

Ironically, the practitioners of all faiths are doing just the opposite.

That is the less than wholesome contribution of organized religion, a subject that I have explored in depth in the chapter that follows this one.

Faith, any faith, is a set of principles supported by a set of beliefs based on the teachings of the founder of the faith. Believers of any new faith are drawn to the faith more by the personality of the founding preacher than by the principles which the faith preaches. A few generations after the founding of the faith, two things happen; first, the faith becomes part of the identity of the faithful and a second nature to them; and, second, the personality of the founder of the faith and some great preachers and teachers who followed him in teaching, explaining, expanding and enforcing the faith assume greater importance than the principles of the faith; the words of the founder and his prominent followers begin to be revered for their sound rather than their substance.

Many are born into the families of the believers and are taught their faith during their formative years by their parents. They are born into the faith and grow up with the ownership of the faith and with an attachment to it. Over time the faith begins to change and transform into something different from the teachings of the original preacher and begin to be institutionalized as a set of traditions and rules according to how they were defined by later interpreters of the faith who began to insert their own understanding and meaning into the faith which the original preacher may or may not have intended.

Self-appointed faith leaders in later times assume more authority in defining the details of the faith, and fairly often significantly change the perspective of the faith or religion.

Faith is the search for the Ultimate Truth. The Ultimate Truth is universal and unique. It does not belong to an individual nor does it belong to a particular group. It belongs to the entire humanity; to each and every member of the human race without regard to where on earth they are born or what group they belong to or what human characteristics they possess.

Organized Faith is founded on the premise of having discovered the Ultimate Truth, and each Organized Faith makes that claim. Each Organized Faith not only declares that it has the right to define that Ultimate Truth in its own special way but also that it has the right to make an exclusive claim to its ownership. All Faiths strive for salvation, but each Organized Faith is adamant that salvation is available exclusively to those who join their ranks and follow their exclusive definition of faith. All others are declared to be condemned and destined to doom. When each organized faith is making the same claim, one wonders whose claim, or if anyone's claim, will accomplish fruition and success.

It is amazing and incredible to find that followers of each of a large number of faiths are adamant in their conviction about the unique righteousness of their own faith and the absolute wrongness of each and every other faith. They hold such a position when they are likely to be fairly ignorant of the content of the other faiths because they rarely make any attempt to learn about them. Immersed in the bliss of their ignorance, they are perfectly willing and happy to condemn everyone else. They are so proud to display the mentality of a pond frog. They isolate themselves within their narrow sphere and loudly deny the existence of anything worthwhile outside their circle.

Any who claims to belong to and practice a faith also claims to believe in a supreme power, a super entity that they hold is the cause and the source of all creation. That superpower is also held to be responsible for designing and establishing the order by which the creation operates, and for establishing the rules and the regulations – the Laws of Nature – under which the creation is supposed to operate. Each group claims exclusive right to define the meanings of those Laws of Nature.

Salvation & Eschatology are human desires dreamed up during troubling times caused by deprivation, torment or oppression. The dreamers chart out a pleasant scenario for themselves and a horrible punishment for all the rest, especially those whom they consider to be responsible for their troubles. Those in positions of power seldom think about eschatological times because for them salvation has already been achieved and is at hand which they are enjoying. And these powerful people do not have to wait for eschatological times to inflict punishment on their enemies; they can and are doing it now.

Looking in from the outside, without giving up one's chosen faith and without pointing a finger of condemnation on any other faith but looking at their tenets and teachings with an open mind and with respect, one finds so much good, so much wisdom and so much beauty in all of them. One comes across, every now and then, a really inspiring statement made by some great personality, of a faith different from one's own faith, in the past or even in the present. One admires its beauty and is awed by the wisdom contained in it. If the person making that discovery, then reaches into their own Holy Scripture with an objective open-minded approach of a seeker of knowledge and wisdom, who holds no preconceived notion of what he or she would find, one may discover that the same statement, containing the same wisdom and inspiration, is there in their own Scripture. That begs the question: why was the Scripture not studied in the first place to seek such wisdom and guidance, rather than being pleasantly surprised by the confirmation in the Scripture of something, anything, that was first learned from another source? The answer to that question is so simple that it is disturbing to the mind that is searching for meaning.

With very few exceptions, most of us do not study our own Holy Books for knowledge or guidance. We just read them as a matter of faith. We read them to seek justification and reinforcement for our strongly held prejudicial convictions and notions. Most of our traditions forbid idol worship, but the way we approach our Holy Books, we have practically turned them into idols, which we then routinely worship. There is little difference between standing before an idol made of wood or stone or clay, and reading Scripture without proper comprehension. One cannot interact with the idol because the idol cannot understand what the worshipper is saying or seeking or asking, and the idol cannot answer either in a verbal manner or a non-verbal way. Reading the Scripture with blind devotion is akin to the forbidden worship of the idol. There is no difference between the worship of an idol and the worship of a Holy Book recited without comprehension, just to gain Blessings.

People who believe in God may not get along with each other. But they believe in God and some of them may even worship God in their own many different ways. Then there are those who do not believe in God at all. Believers in God may call them Atheists, and some of them may even gladly agree with that label.

Atheism is just the opposite of Theism. This word is derived from the Greek word Theos, which comes from Sanskrit word Deva, meaning God or the spirit of God. The atheists either have no concept of deities or deny a creator deity or revere some other god-like entities. Most atheists may just simply be following some different traditions and as such they may be believers of some entity or idea or system of cultural values. But the concepts they follow may be seen by the followers of organized religions as unacceptable to them; so, they may declare them to be atheists. This has been a common practice of humans throughout history. Any people whose belief systems may be different from the prevailing custom, are often designated as atheists. As Karen Armstrong observed, "Atheism has often been a transitional state: thus Jews, Christians and Muslims were all called 'atheists' by their pagan contemporaries because they had adopted a revolutionary notion of divinity and transcendence. Is modern atheism a similar denial of a God which is no longer adequate to the problems of our time?"[1]

---

[1] Karen Armstrong: A History of God, page 13-14.

Of particular interest to this enquiry are those highly educated people who claim their lack of belief in God or their open declaration that there is no God, on the basis of their advanced knowledge. They have undertaken scientific enquiry, done scholarly research and made philosophical analysis, which led them to the conclusion that there is no God. According to Karen Armstrong, "Science seemed to have disposed of the Creator God"[2]. These highly educated men and women may not believe in God, but most of them, if not all, are not divisive and hostile to each other or even to those who believe in God, including those faithful people who may look ill towards these highly educated atheists. These educated atheists are generally, though not necessarily always, easy to get along with.

One can ask me as to where I stand. I will willingly answer. I believe in God. The same scientific enquiry, scholarly research and philosophical analysis, which led many to reach the conclusion that there was no God, actually convinced me that there is God. I will explain it with the caveat that this reasoning is only for me because it finds acceptance and satisfaction with me. Nobody who reads this should find themselves under any obligation to accept it, or even to consider it.

Sumerians had developed a creation theory a long time ago. Then the writers of Bible created another similar theory and described it in the first chapter of the Book of Genesis. Sumerians declared that earth and sky were created from the body of Tiamat and humans were created from the blood of Kingu for the specific purpose of serving gods so the divines may be free of the need to work. Sumerians placed no timeline on the process of creation. Bible places a time period of six days on that process, and each day's creation is defined step by step in detail. Sumerians believed in a Divine Pantheon headed by Marduk. Genesis in Bible believes in One God and promotes monotheism. Human creation took place on the sixth day with God making a figure from clay and blowing life into it. "Then the LORD God formed a man from the dust of the ground and breathed into his nostrils the breath of life."[3] God finished the creation in six days and "on the seventh day he rested".[4] The essence of the Sumerian human was the blood of Kingu. The essence of the Biblical human is the spirit of God.

---

[2] Karen Armstrong: A History of God, page 11.
[3] Genesis 2:7.
[4] Genesis 2:2.

The Quranic statement about creation of universe is in one sentence, repeated more than once; it does mention six days but does not mention the day of rest. "We have indeed created the heavens and the earth and all that is between them in six eons, and no weariness could ever touch Us." (Quran 50:38 – Asad Translation) Creation of man is similar to what Bible describes. "I have formed him fully and breathed into him of My spirit."[5]

Bible provides a timeline from one generation to next starting from the first man Adam. The Quran does not provide such a timeline. Biblical timeline facilitates a calculation of the time since Biblical creation. Two Biblical researchers are well known for establishing the date of creation. John Lightfoot (1602-1675) calculated it to be September 17, 3928 BC, which would make the earth to be 5,949 years old on September 17, 2021. James Ussher (1581-1656) calculated it to be around 6 pm on 22 October 4004 BC, which would make the earth 6,025 years old on 22 October 2021.

Human knowledge has gone way beyond the Biblical timeline of the creation of universe and earth. It is now believed that the universe was not created around 6,000 years ago, as deduced from Bible, but almost 14 billion years ago. Human knowledge has now grown to a level that enables the people of knowledge, not only to ascertain the age of universe and its various components, but also enables the scientists to theoretically explain – or at least place a timeline on – the entire process of creation and evolution, step by step.

According to the Big Bang Theory – one of the theories of the origin of universe – the entire vastness of the universe, and all of its matter and radiation, consisted of a mass a few millimeters across, a tiny bundle of energy. The history of the universe began mysteriously. For reasons we as yet do not know and may never know, our universe suddenly erupted within a fraction of a second. The big bang created all of the energy that would ever exist. That explosion created our universe some 13.7 billion years ago.

Humans have been seeking knowledge to gain an understanding of their existence and their surroundings for a very long time. They have also been searching for meaning of life and the meaning of the very existence of everything and have been wondering about the source of it all. That quest has always led humans to the idea of God as the source of life. Sumerian civilization existed in Mesopotamia, the lower part of the Tigris-Euphrates

---

[5] Quran 15:29 – Asad Translation.

valley, from before 4000 BCE to around 2000 BCE. They had developed an idea of the supreme entity that created the universe and life. According to their thinking, the divine emerged first who was not one but many, both male and female, whose unions created successive generations of gods. Finally, the mighty Marduk, the most perfect god, emerged and took control of all existence in the universe. According to the Sumerian thinking, all heavenly bodies, such as the heavens and the earth and the sun, were all gods. Sun being the most visible and the most powerful, it became identified with Marduk who became the Sun God. After the gods had existed for some time and had built the great ziggurat of Babylon as the seat of the power of Marduk, the Sun God, the humans were created. Marduk killed Kingu, the god, and mixed his divine blood with the dust of the Earth to shape the first man. Thus, having been created from the substance of a god, man shared the divine nature. The biblical story of creation is very similar. It could be taken to begin with Abraham who began to wonder about the source of creation. According to Qur'an, when Abraham was searching for the ultimate reality, he first wondered about stars, then moon and finally the sun as the possible source of all creation. But when each set after rising, he concluded that the ultimate reality and the source of all creation had to be superior to all of them. Then over a thousand years later a theory was developed and written down another thousand years after its development. Whether it was God, who told it to the men, or the men who thought of it themselves, or it was influenced by the Sumerian ideas, that theory was put in the Genesis and later into the Qur'an. It placed a time frame on creation by specifying that God did it in six days. According to Genesis, on the sixth day God formed the man out of dust and breathed into his nostrils the breath of life. Man in this theory also shares the divine nature through a divine substance, the Breath of God. Genesis makes certain that six days are understood to be six regular days by meticulously defining them as 24-hour days of our current human reckoning. Then Genesis and other Books of Bible place a definite timeline on the progress of humanity and the universe; universe being 5 days older than the humanity. Qur'an does state that God created the heavens and the earth in six days[6], but then goes on to define the "day" under multiple circumstances as a long period of time rather than a 24-hour day.

---

[6] Quran 7:54; 10:3; 11:7; 25:59; 32:4; 50:38; 57:4.

The Arabic word Yaum, which is also a Hebrew word, and its plural Ayyam can be used for regular 24-hour days or for periods of any length, such as eon or epoch. Qur'an uses Yaum for 1,000 years in 22:47 and 32:5 and for 50,000 years in 70:4. Qur'an is silent about universal age as well as human timeline. It does not indicate how old the universe is or how long it took to be created except to state that it was created in six days, which could mean six stages of varying lengths of time. A reader of the Qur'an can feel free to interpret it as six 24-hour days, as many, including Muslims, have done, or can take it to mean something else.

Qur'an also goes on to describe the creation of the first human from dust or clay, into whom God breathed his spirit. From that one man, He created his wife, and from the two were created the multitude of humanity. "Thy Sustainer said unto the angels: 'Behold, I am about to create a human being out of clay: and when I have formed him fully and breathed into him of My spirit, fall you down before him in prostration!'"[7] Thus Quran also indicates that humans have Divine substance, the Spirit of God, and all humans are the progeny those two humans. "O MANKIND! Be conscious of your Sustainer, who has created you out of one living entity, and out of it created its mate, and out of the two spread abroad a multitude of men and women."[8]

It was a pretty good theory from the standpoint of the level of human knowledge at that time. Earlier than that, the Hindus had theorized that Brahma was responsible, not only for the initial creation of the universe, but also for every later re-creation, each time he found it necessary to destroy it. There might be other theories because there had been so many knowledgeable civilizations. Most of those theories assumed the earth to be the center of the universe. Some may also have assumed earth to be flat. Over the next couple of thousand years human knowledge grew tremendously and enabled humans to gain a better understanding. We know a lot more now, but we still do not know everything. We are still learning. That old theory stipulated that the world was populated beginning with two human individuals. Current theory believes that it started with 200 individuals. Both are plausible. The future will bring even better knowledge.

---

[7] Quran 38:71-72.
[8] Quran 4:1.

When we trace back from our time to the beginning of time, we find that we have learned a lot and are able to explain many stages of creation and evolution, putting dates and time periods on things and processes. We have gained an understanding of many things, and we continue to strive for answers to as yet unanswered questions. We accept that while we may answer some of the questions, there may be some that we might never be able to answer. When we go back all the way to the big bang, we believe that it began with the explosion of a mass that was only a few millimeters across, a tiny bundle of energy. Those with knowledge freely admit that the history of the universe began mysteriously because, for reasons we may never know, our universe suddenly erupted within a fraction of a second. While the process with which the creation of the universe began is still an unresolved mystery, there is another question that is frequently overlooked and even less frequently asked. That question is about that small mass, the tiny bundle of energy, which is believed to have exploded with the big bang. Where did that mass come from? What was its source? Who or what was responsible for its creation? Science has established that things can only be created by starting with some kind of an existing material. A small seed can be planted into earth, and it will grow into a plant, a small plant or even a huge tree. Chemical processes can transform one type of element or material or combinations of two or more elements into entirely new products. A mass only a few millimeters across, a tiny bundle of energy, can explode into the universe. But something is always needed to create something else. It is not possible to create something out of nothing. It is not possible to create a perpetual machine. That small mass which exploded into the universe by big bang, had to have a source.

Until such time when people of scientific knowledge can come up with some other reasonably plausible explanation for the source of that mass, to me that source is God. Someone could raise the question, 'where did God come from?' That question is way beyond my pay grade.

Once I accept God, I would proceed to declare that I believe that the creative power of God is responsible for all the processes and stages of creation and all the transformations and changes that our modern superior knowledge has enabled us to observe but as yet is unable to explain.

Humans possess intellect which enables them to observe and analyze. Analysis is the motivated by the human curiosity and the desire to understand what has been observed. Over time humans have continued to strive to develop tools and methods to analyze observed phenomena. Perhaps the quest began with Abraham who observed the heavenly bodies and attempted to establish their relationship to the mysterious creation of humans and their environment. Or it may have begun even before Abraham. Or with someone else. Ever since that first human – whoever that might be – wondered about what he/she observed and tried to find some meaning in it, the quest has been going on.

Over time that quest and its methods and tools have grown better and ever more sophisticated. They have by now become very good and will continue to improve even further. Persons of special talent and skill have long been building a treasure of knowledge and a huge set of tools and methods. But the Biblical idea of the creation and the age of universe was the only source of information for a long time; it placed the age of universe around 6,000 years.

A maverick Scottish farmer named James Hutton (1726-1797) made an astounding discovery in 1788 and changed the entire thinking on the age of universe. On a small rocky hilltop near the Edinburgh coast of Scotland, he discovered that rocks are formed from sediment over a very long period of time – hundreds of thousands or maybe millions of years. That led to the techniques of estimating the age of rocks. From the layers of rocks in the rock formation it became possible not only to age the hill but also to understand the process of its formation.

The radiometric dating process enabled the scientists to accurately calculate the age of the earth. Other methods were discovered and developed such as the rings of tree trunks and layers of ice in glaciers. These and many other methods not only provided the ability to check the ages of things on earth, and finally of the earth itself, but they also provided the ability to verify the calculations by comparing the results from various different methods. Having gained knowledge of the age of the earth, quest continued to calculate the age of our solar system and the age of the universe. More sophisticated methods were developed to accomplish that.

Once the speed of light was known, astronomical observations made it possible to calculate the time that the light from various observable objects took to reach the earth, thereby finding the age of those objects. It is possible, but not necessarily easy. Astronomers use several different but related methods to determine the distances, such as geometric calculations and brightness measurements. Galaxies are expanding and moving apart.

The speed of their movement is not constant, but it follows a certain pattern. A precise understanding of that pattern enables the scientists to make accurate measurements of distances through time the light took to reach earth. Using careful measurements of the change in its expansion rate, the age of the universe has been calculated to be 13.7 billion years.

Fossils are dated by radiometric dating processes. Carbon dating process can be used on organic materials less than 50,000 years old. When fossils of old living, but now extinct, life forms are found they can be dated using these methods. That helps humans to know exactly when the various different living things existed. It is known, for example, that dinosaurs lived on earth from about 230 million years before our time until about 65 million years ago.

Homo erectus is believed to have lived between 2 million years ago to about 300,000 years before now. Similarly, fossil analysis has enabled scientists to place beginning and ending dates on all life forms that existed in the past on earth, and whose fossils have been found, even though these life forms are extinct now. Humans also have been able to develop theories about some of the characteristics of these living things and their life cycles. That is a great achievement. Most of this knowledge has been gained in very recent times; as recent as the 21st Century. But it is still mostly a mystery as to how these life forms came into being or transformed from one form to another. Scientists have developed theories about the evolution of one life form into another. It is theorized, for example, that the fish came out of water on to land and evolved into tetrapod by transforming its fins into legs and growing two more legs. This process took a very long time, perhaps millions of years. But it is not known as yet, and may never be known, exactly how that happened.

Human knowledge now is immensely greater than it was only a short time ago. In recent times there has been an explosion of human knowledge of the proportions of the big bang that initiated the universe. The extent of the current knowledge and its continued rapid growth, gives humans confidence that, in time, it will become possible to understand and explain everything. But the fact remains that while the current level of knowledge is tremendous, the extent of what is not known and is not yet possible to explain is also just as immense, maybe even greater.

But the confidence from what humans have already been able to accomplish has led a number of people of knowledge – scientists, scholars, philosophers – to conclude that perhaps everything happens in the universe by some as yet unexplained self-operating internal process without any interference from an external source. These people of knowledge have decided to separate themselves from those who hold that these processes are caused and to an extent controlled by an external source called God.

Their current knowledge and their confidence in the future growth of knowledge appears to have inspired them to declare that 'Science seemed to have disposed of the Creator God', in the words of Karen Armstrong quoted before. Those who follow the God of Religion insist that these people of knowledge are wrong. The religious people, who may not hesitate to avail themselves of all the benefits and conveniences and luxuries created by the scientific advancements, continue to defiantly reject even such findings of science which are self-evident in nature around them, as long as it contradicts their strongly held views and beliefs.

The result is another debate that is not very different from all the debates which have raged throughout the human history between various religions. Now science, to some people, has become yet another religion and some, but not all, of its advocates have taken just as rigid a position in their advocacy as the preachers of any religion ever did.

What is the source of this conflict? Why can the people not agree to listen to each other and find the similarities and common ground which clearly exist between their various positions? What is preventing them from coming together to find that common ground? Could it be the human ego that is keeping them apart and keeping them locked up in a debate which is more destructive than beneficial?

Religion has dominated human society for a long time; perhaps ever since humans came on earth. The religious authority controlled the actions and thoughts of people and insisted on deciding every aspect of human behavior. Any who dared to challenge the prevailing religious doctrine paid dearly, sometime with their life. Examples of Spinoza, Galileo Galilei, Martin Luther, and all the Christian martyrs under Roman Catholic persecution are well known. In some parts of the world, religious authority is not that dominant anymore, but in other parts, religion continues to decide the fate of the people. Spinoza was punished for attempting to redefine God, but at least that right has now been acquired and is available to anyone who chooses to use it. Perhaps as a reaction to the long held controlling authority of religion, some of those who have chosen to exercise that right have gone to the other extreme, complete denial of the very existence of God. They base this claim on science by declaring that science has disposed of the idea of God. It is possible that at some future date, with knowledge advanced to a much higher level than its current level, science may acquire an understanding of the creative power of nature and be able to explain how the mass that exploded into the universe came into existence by itself, out of nothing. But as yet science has not done that.

It can be acknowledged that science is not in the business of proving or disproving the existence of God. It is a matter of faith, for which there cannot be scientific or mathematical proof. For that matter, religion can also not prove that there is God beyond a matter of faith. And for faith, no proof is necessary; one either believes or does not believe. But there are people who make claims and declarations using religion or science as authority. Karen Armstrong made that claim in her famous "The History of God" that science has disposed of the idea of a creative God. But that statement should not be made because there is no validity for it. The idea of some entity that has the power of creating something out of nothing, create life and cause species to evolve into increasingly complex life forms remain undisposed. Acknowledgement of the existence of such an entity – call it God or something else – does not necessarily validate the right of the religious authority to compel people to submit to that authority's prescription of human behavior. From the recognition of the creative power of God, it does not necessarily follow that God wants to control every minute of our life and would appoint some human authority to ensure that we would obey. As of now science has not shown exactly what created the material from which the universe exploded, how it exploded, how various systems and processes came into operation, and how life came into being and evolved so many times. Science has so far been able to observe the existence of the many heavenly bodies, theorize very nicely about their interrelation, observe the existence of life in many forms, and observe the many cycles of evolution of life, from one species to another. As yet science has not come to an understanding of creative power and the causes of evolution. What science has learned so far is simply enormous and mind boggling but is not yet enough to establish that things happen without cause and without someone or something controlling that cause. Therefore, the idea of a Creative God has not yet been disposed. But at the same time, the idea of a God who is involved in the life of humans on an ongoing basis –

dictating and controlling and judging continuously – has also not been established.

It is possible to question the idea of organized religion that gives some humans the right to assume authority over human behavior and force people to conform to their dictates. Having questioned the idea of organized religion, it is possible to discard it after due research. I will examine this subject in the next discourse.

So, I join those who believe in God, but they are not likely to accept me. They will most probably reject me with the same contempt with which they have always rejected the atheists and have rejected each other.

# 2. Organized Religion: Its Role and Need

*Organized religions have used the scriptures through ever ingenious interpretations and innovations, coupled with powerful enforcement using religious authority claimed in the name of God. Such abuses have given rise to divisiveness and hostilities within humanity whereas God clearly ordains social harmony. The stakeholders of organized religions block this harmony.*

People of faith constantly speak of the mercy of God and compassion of God. Often it is referred to as the grace of God. The Hebrew word for mercy is Rachamim, which is in the plural, meaning mercies. Its Hebrew root word is Racham which means 'womb', from which the meaning of mercy is derived, because no one displays more mercy than a mother. Mercy of mother is believed to be exceeded only by mercy of God. The more common meaning of Racham would be compassion. The Arabic root word is the same as that in Hebrew, Raham, with the same pronunciation as the Hebrew word, but with a slightly different transliteration method in English. The meaning of the Arabic root word is also 'womb'. From this word are derived two Arabic words, Rahman and Rahim, translated into English as compassionate and merciful, respectively, though endowed with richer meanings in its original Arabic. Gita refers to God as the shelter of the universe.

Bible speaks of the mercy or grace of God in many places.[1]

Qur'an also speaks of mercy or grace of God repeatedly. The most prominent mention is in the Fateha, the Opening Chapter. That chapter begins by declaring that all praise is for God who is the Cherisher and

---

[1] 2 Chronicles 30:9, Hebrews 4:13-16, John 3:16-17, Luke 1:50, Deut. 7:9, Deut. 4:31, and Nehemiah 9:27.

Sustainer of all the worlds, is Compassionate/Gracious (Rahman) and is Merciful (Rahim), is the Lord of the Final Judgment. That is followed by a confession and ends with a supplication.

When it comes to the attributes of God, and several are mentioned in the first or opening chapter of the Quran, faith requires the believer to accept and confess to all, or at least confess to most of them. Cherisher, Sustainer, Lord of the Final Judgment, Ruler of the entire universe, are all attributes that are easy to accept and confess to. But when it comes to Rahman meaning Gracious (which can also be termed as Kind or Compassionate) and Rahim meaning Merciful, one has to pause to decide if to accept and confess to them. These are human qualities, and it may not be possible to apply them to God. The human experience throughout human history does not support these qualities as attributes of God; at least not in the same sense as these qualities are applied and understood in human terms.

Abdullah Yusuf Ali appears to make the same point when he states that: "The Arabic intensive is more suited to express God's attributes than the superlative degree in English. The latter implies a comparison with other beings, or with other times or places, while there is no being like unto God, and He is independent of Time and Place". He explains the difference between Rahman and Rahim. "Mercy may imply pity, long-suffering, patience, and forgiveness, all of which the sinner needs and God Most Merciful bestows in abundant measure. But there is a Mercy that goes before even the need arises, the Grace, which is ever watchful, and flows from Rahman, God Most Gracious, to all His creatures, protecting them, preserving them, guiding them, and leading them to clearer light and higher life. For this reason, the attribute Rahman (Most Gracious) is not applied to any but God, but the attribute Rahim (Merciful), is a general term, and may also be applied to Men."[2]

There is a problem here and some kind of a contradiction which needs to be resolved. If Grace of God, implicit in His attribute as Rahman, is ever present, even before someone performs an act, any act, good or bad, for which Rahman is forever protecting, preserving, guiding and leading His creatures to clearer light and higher life, then, in the light of the unlimited and boundless power of God and his Absolute control over everyone and everything, no one would ever do anything against His Will or His Law. But

---

[2] Abdullah Yusuf Ali, Translation of The Quran, Chapter 1, Al-Fateha, Note 19.

we see such things happening all the time. Perhaps they are part of His plan; and that operating plan is allowing them to happen, or even causing them to happen. It requires a lot of thought and analysis. Human insistence that God is involved in our life on an ongoing basis, to judge our every action and to immediately reward or punish us, is incompatible with the observed reality.

God cannot be constantly involved in human life; He cannot care what we do. God is aloof and is letting his creatures have and enjoy complete freedom to live their mortal life any way they please. The miseries and calamities constantly being faced by the humanity are not only possible to explain but also become easy to accept if we make God aloof from human life and not interfering in it or controlling it on an ongoing basis.

It is also hard to explain why both Quran and Bible blame humans for not following the Divine guidance.

"Enter through the narrow gate. For wide is the gate and broad is the road that leads to destruction, and many enter through it. But small is the gate and narrow the road that leads to life, and only a few find it."[3]

"Show us the straight way. The Way of those whom You have favored; not of those who have earned Your wrath, or of those who have lost The Way."[4]

Why would both Qur'an and Gospel talk about the narrow and broad path and then lament that humans generally follow the broad path to destruction and shun the narrow path to salvation and success? Why does God have to complain about human behavior when God is so all-powerful that, if He so chose, He could control human behavior? Are the humans not expressing their own frustrations in the speech of God, who may not, and most probably does not care about human conduct at all? God has created the people, given them a broad range of abilities and skills and endowed them with free will to use those abilities any way they please. He has completed the creation, has set in place a system of nature that operates according to the rules which He instituted, and now he does not interfere in human activities and human behavior.

---

[3] Matthew 7:13-14
[4] Quran 1:6-7

Even when people pray, the prayer is not to invoke an action by God; it is just for reaching into one's own inner self to motivate one's own latent capabilities to overcome the self-created difficulties.

All of this is built into the human personality. "Consider the human soul and how it has been designed. It has been inspired to distinguish between wrong and right. Those who purify it will succeed. And those who corrupt it will fail".[5] Humans are born with built-in knowledge of how to live on earth.

Qur'an says more clearly what other scriptures also imply that God is free of all needs, even the need of praise or supplication from humans. He is above caring for anything that humans would ever do, good or bad. Whatever happens to humans, whether it helps and benefits them or hurts and harms them, is their own doing. They succeed on their own and fail on their own, without any interference from God in their day-to-day life and activities.

Yaum-al-Deen, Day of Judgment, reckoning or recompense always leads to a discussion of reward and punishment. The idea of punishment is problematic. There is no problem in accepting that God will judge people and grade them according to His Judgment of their performance in their mortal life. After they die, if there is an afterlife, God will judge their performance in their mortal life, taking into account all the extraneous circumstances, and reward them an afterlife compatible with His judgment. His award would vary in accordance with his judgment; some will be compensated with better rewards than others. But no one would actually be punished with any kind of torment. Even if there is an afterlife, there is not likely to be a heaven or a hell as described in the Book of Revelation or in the Qur'an. It would just be one domain in which people will begin normal – good or better life – as rewarded by God. From that start they can then improve or deteriorate, as is common for human behavior.

There is not going to be any lake of fire.

Worship is another concept that needs to be visited with a great deal of thought. Abdullah Yusuf Ali states that "we bend in the act of worship and see both our shortcomings and His all-sufficient power"[6]. That may be a reference to the Muslim method of worship or a general statement about

---

[5] Quran 91:7-10.
[6] Abdullah Yusuf Ali, Translation of The Quran, Chapter 1, Al-Fateha, Note 21.

being subservient to God. But the path is open to define worship in a more meaningful, hopefully universal, way. Muslims use the Arabic word Salah – or Salat in its Urdu and Farsi pronunciation – as the concept of required worship and then insist on its prescribed method and timings.

The root word of Salah is Sallun, which simply means to connect or to communicate. Humans have always felt the need to connect with God. They have devised a myriad of methods to accomplish it, including making representations of God in human or animal shapes. There is nothing wrong with many different methods of connecting with God, in different parts of the world and in different cultures. As long as each group is happy and satisfied in the practice of their chosen method, the goal is accomplished.

Problem arises when the practitioners of each method lay an exclusive claim to the exclusive righteousness of their own method, openly and loudly condemn all other methods and begin to demand that everyone else should abandon every other "wrong" method to adopt their "only and exclusively righteous" method. And they all become so insistent on their own exclusive and unique righteousness, and their strong condemnation of everyone else, that it becomes divisive and hostile.

The goal is to connect with God, and everyone can use their own chosen method to make that connection. That is the universally meaningful way to connect with God, without an assertion about the rightness or wrongness of the methods of worship others use. The problem is that the organized religion stands in the way of this universal way. Organized religion is a source of conflict, as are its sacrosanct rituals for connecting with God.

Ancient Egyptians believed in a Pantheon with Ra as the chief god presiding over many other gods. There was one Pharaoh who believed in monotheism and attempted to institute the idea of One God. That was Akhenaten (1353-1336 BCE), the tenth ruler of the Eighteenth Dynasty.

The point is dramatically made in the 2014 movie 'Exodus: Gods and Kings', directed by Ridley Scott. The priest assigned to educate young Moses, when he was growing up as Prince of Egypt, told Moses about an idea of Akhenaten, and then ridiculed it in the following way. "The Pharaoh Akhenaten said there wasn't one god for Egypt and other gods for other people. If the idea of God had any meaning, there could only be one all-powerful God." Having asserted this, the priest told Moses that it was not a good idea. He argued, "But if men started to question what they had been told to believe since the world began, what else might they not begin to question? One God! It is a ridiculous idea! Far better that there should be as many gods as there are men, if only to keep us priests employed".

That is the essence of the organized religion; the vested interest of those who benefit from it. In order to protect and promote their vested self-interest, they vigorously promote their own idea of God, and the idea of their prescribed sacrosanct ritualistic worship. Whether God cares about these ideas is not the issue; what is paramount is the self-interest of the stakeholders. They justify their position with creative and specialized treatments of the scriptures. Such treatments overwhelmingly overrule even the most highly scholastic reading of God and His scriptures if that does not agree with their own. An objective reading of the scriptures finds no requirement for any sacrosanct ritualistic worship.

Organized religion, controlled by vested interests, creates so much friction that it becomes counterproductive, if not outright dangerous. All Faiths strive for salvation, but each organized faith is adamant that salvation is available exclusively to those who join their ranks and follow their exclusive definition of faith and their chosen method of worship. All others are declared to be apocryphal and destined to doom. When each organized faith is making the same claim, one wonders whose claim, or if anyone's claim, will actually accomplish fruition and success.

Organized religion is founded on dogma, promulgated and promoted by the religious authority as the ultimate truth: the dogma is manmade but made sacrosanct in the name of the Devine. The religious authority, acting in the name of the Devine, requires and enforces the dogma at all costs, demanding that it should be followed at all times and never to be violated. That self-appointed authority grants itself an enormous power to demand total submission and complete conformity with the dogma. Violators are subject to severe punishment, even death.

Galileo Galilei (1564-1642) was condemned by the Catholic Church of "vehement suspicion of heresy" for his support of Copernicus' theory of heliocentrism. He was sentenced to prison, later commuted to house arrest, for the final eight years of his life. His writings were banned, and all future publications were forbidden. This is how organized religion imposes dogma to suffocate pursuit of knowledge.

Ahmad Bin Hanbal (780-855) refused to submit to the dogma accepted and promoted by the Abbasi rulers of his time. He was repeatedly imprisoned, put in chains and flogged.

Baruch Spinoza (1632-1677) was excommunicated by the Talmud Torah Congregation of Amsterdam for his "evil opinions and acts", his "wicked ways", his "abominable heresies", and "his monstrous deeds". He was "expelled from the people of Israel" with this pronouncement: "By the decree of the angels, and by the command of the holy men, we excommunicate, expel, curse and damn Baruch de Espinoza, with the consent of God". It is not clear how the consent of God and the decree of the angels were obtained, but the self-appointed guardians of faith never feel any obligation to answer such questions.

Spanish theologian, Michael Servetus (1511-1553) was denounced as heretic by both Catholic and Protestant authorities, including John Calvin. He was accused of being opposed to Trinity and Infant Baptism. He was suspected to favor Jews and Turks (meaning Muslims) and was accused of having studied the Koran. He was found guilty of denying the Trinity and infant baptism and was burnt alive, atop a pyre of his own books. The role of John Calvin was considered troublesome by Lord Acton[7], who speaks of it as the defining moment of Calvin's life. "A man is hanged not because he can or cannot prove his claim to virtues," explains Acton, "but because it can be proved that he has committed a particular crime. That one action overshadows the rest of his career." Lord Acton concludes: "We all agree that Calvin was one of the greatest writers, many think him the best religious teacher, in the world. But that one affair of Servetus outweighs the nine folios, and settles, by itself, the reputation he deserves."[8]

Many other renowned men have participated in and contributed to the persecution of countless victims of the weaponization of the authority vested in an organized religion. Organized religion continues to control human life even today with dictates of what to believe and what not to believe; with demands to conform to these dictates at the pain of severe condemnation and punishment. These leaders of the organized religion have by and large been able to preserve their reputation, just as has Calvin, in spite of the isolated criticism from some people like Lord Acton.

---

[7] John Emerich Edward Dalberg-Acton, 1st Baron Acton, 13th Marquess of Groppoli, (1834-1902), better known as Lord Acton, was an English Catholic historian, politician, and writer. He is best remembered for the remark he wrote in a letter to an Anglican bishop in 1887.

[8] "The Protestant Theory of Persecution," (1862)

Those vested in the authority derived from organized religion, hold that authority to be legitimate and sacred, and defend it with all their power. Archbishop Creighton had taken such a position which Lord Acton found to be not worthy of the position of a Bishop. Lord Acton wrote to Archbishop Creighton; "you say that people in authority are not [to] be snubbed or sneezed at from our pinnacle of conscious rectitude. I really don't know whether you exempt them because of their rank, or of their success and power, or of their date." Then Lord Acton goes on to address the real problem with organized religion. "I cannot accept your canon that we are to judge Pope and King unlike other men, with a favorable presumption that they did no wrong. If there is any presumption, it is the other way against holders of power, increasing as the power increases. Historic responsibility has to make up for the want of legal responsibility. Power tends to corrupt and absolute power corrupts absolutely. Great men are almost always bad men, even when they exercise influence and not authority: still more when you superadd the tendency or the certainty of corruption by authority. There is no worse heresy than that the office sanctifies the holder of it. That is the point at which the negation of Catholicism and the negation of Liberalism meet and keep high festival, and the end learns to justify the means. You would hang a man of no position, like Ravaillac[9]; but if what one hears is true, then Elizabeth asked the gaoler to murder Mary, and William III ordered his Scottish minister to extirpate a clan. Here are the greater names coupled with the greater crimes. You would spare these criminals, for some mysterious reason. I would hang them, higher than Haman, for reasons of quite obvious justice; still more, still higher, for the sake of historical science."[10]

Lord Acton pinpoints the essential flaw of organized religion when he denounces its position that "the office sanctifies the holder of it".

People tend to be so firmly indoctrinated with the dogma of 'office sanctifies the holder of it' that if someone, troubled by a rare push of realization, attempts to make amends, those around him would make a concerted effort to dissuade him. The 1949 RKO movie 'Adventure in Baltimore' directed by Richard Wallace, deals with this phenomenon.

---

[9] Francois Ravaillac (1578-1610) was a French Catholic zealot who assassinated King Henry IV of France in 1610.
[10] Lord Acton's Letter to Bishop Mandell Creighton, April 5, 1887.

Robert Young is playing an Episcopalian pastor under consideration for the position of Bishop. His family is the subject of community outrage because of his daughter's nonconforming behavior, including advocating for women's rights. Even though he was trying to shield his daughter because he was not sure how to assess her behavior, he had now realized that his daughter had done nothing wrong. He wanted to defend her from the pulpit, but his associates were strongly opposed and urged him to remain silent so as not to jeopardize his chances to become Bishop. His response; "Well, of course, if I weren't concerned about becoming Bishop and if I weren't willing to just forget the whole thing, I would have a few things to say, few points to make. To begin with, I would very proudly contend that my family stood up and fought for the rights of a group of individuals." Everyone in his inner circle was shocked by this assertion of the Pastor and pleaded with him not to say anything like that. He would admit that "I was willing to submit because I was concerned about my possible election as Bishop." Then he continued; "If what my family and I have done is wrong, then I do not deserve to be Bishop. The only important thing is that unless I say these things, I am not serving my congregation and the first obligation a minister has, is to serve. I can only serve by speaking the truth." He continued; "I shall probably say something about the way we use words like meanness and intolerance and bigotry but, somehow, we manage to use them with connection with other people but never with ourselves. What has happened here in last few days, this gossip, is mean, intolerant and bigoted! If it is not pointed out and recognized for what it is, who can say what other kind of cruel thing it may lead to tomorrow? There is no measure of a lie, neither little nor big. It is always a lie. And I don't want to see among people, any man, judge his neighbor. That we must always leave to God." Those who believe in God claim to know what God wants them to do and confidently declare that they are doing it. They claim to know that judgment belongs to God – Judge not, lest ye be judged – but repeatedly forget it when they constantly rise to judge everyone other than themselves and condemn others for things which they declare to be wrong. They themselves might be doing the same things for which they condemn others but would never acknowledge it. The pastor appears to preach for harmony when he walks up to the pulpit and tells the people to make a change from Hymn 127 posted for the day to Hymn 493 which begins; "O brother man, fold to thy heart thy brother."

Truth! Hardly any people ever recognize the truth. And when any do recognize the truth, they are frequently unable or unwilling to speak it for fear of being demonized. This is a movie. Robert Young is not really a pastor, and he is not really up for the position of a Bishop; he is just playing a role. It is easy for him to speak the truth because the writer has written it for him, and the director has taught him how to deliver it. He is just doing a job for which no one will ever demonize him; he will face no consequences. Still, what he says is very meaningful and a true representation of human reality.

There are many examples of people unwilling to speak the truth for fear of being demonized. One such example comes from a tragic situation that happened a few years ago.

During the first invasion of Gaza by Israel, there was tremendous destruction which caused untold misery for the residents of Gaza. An American Jewish Organization named 'Rabbis for Gaza' took intense interest in the situation with sympathy for people of Gaza. Their passion for the situation was very powerful. One of their dispatches said: "Whatever you may think of the respective leadership, Israelis or Hamas, whatever God you may pray to, if you cannot look at Gaza and agree that there is suffering that needs to be alleviated no matter who is to blame for it, then your heart is so dead that tourists flock there." The group came together to draft a position paper in support of Gaza and critical of Israel. After that statement was finalized, it was supposed to be signed by each member of the group. They had freely deliberated in the confines of the group, but now they faced the reality in which this statement would become public and would become known to their congregations. Some of them refused to sign it. Reason? They feared the most certain condemnation of their congregations and were afraid that they would lose their jobs.

That is the power of organized religion, rather its corruption.

When we identify a problem which causes suffering, misery and harm to a large multitude of people, many may recognize it as a problem in need of a solution, but not necessarily everyone. No matter how many people a problem may hurt and harm, there will always be some who benefit from it. Covid-19 has caused untold sufferings for countless people and have caused the death of hundreds of thousands in America alone, and millions worldwide, but there are those who have made billions in profits during, and because of, this horrible pandemic. Those who draw a benefit from a situation, no matter how miserable it is for how many, would not consider it a problem and would strongly oppose any attempt at a solution, because a solution to that problem means a loss of benefit and advantage for them. That is why they would oppose any solution. They would focus on painting a picture which would depict the problematic situation as beneficial and would depict the attempt at a solution to be the real problem. Organized religion provides a prime example of this phenomenon.

Humans have a great ability to rationalize and persuade. Such people would be able to preserve their advantage and benefit, by using their great skills of oratory and persuasion to convince the victims of the problem that they are actually better off under the status quo. The reformers are seldom found to exercise similar persuasion tactics, perhaps because they do not want to engage in this kind of indoctrination. That is why the reformers often fail. When those who benefit from such a problem hold the ultimate power, as does the authority under organized religion, they are successful in preventing a solution, and cause those who may attempt to improve things to fail. Any dissenting voice is simply crushed; recall Servetus, Galileo Galilei, Spinoza, and others.

The basic understanding and guidance for proper conduct in life is already built into the human personality. This is asserted in Quran 91:7-10 which has already been quoted above. Socrates said the same thing about all knowledge being already built into human intellect; all that a human has to do is to remember it or recall it.

Humans can recognize the truths and achieve proper guidance and direction in life on their own, without any help or guidance from organized religion. They can, if they feel the need, seek divine help to supplement their innate wisdom. They can consult scriptures, minus their treatment by the organized religion, to help bring to the conscious level the human knowledge already present in their system but which might be lying dormant within their subconscious.

When we talk about the wrath of God and people going astray, we are imputing to God some human judgment about those whom, for one reason or other, the authorities of the organized religion may not like. The reason for the dislike may have more to do with the organized religion and its authorities, as well as its adherents, than anything in the conduct or behavior of those whom the particular organized religion seeks to condemn to the wrath of God. However, God has no deference for any particular dogma or the stakeholders within an organized religion.

Three major faiths are identified with Abraham: Judaism, Christianity and Islam. All three share the belief that humanity began with Adam and Eve and all humans are their children. This is declared in Bible and in Qur'an. "God formed a man from the dust of the ground and breathed into his nostrils the breath of life".[11] "Then the LORD God made a woman from the rib he had taken out of the man",[12] and "she would become the mother of all the living".[13] Quran declares the same in 49:13. "We have created you all from a male and a female, and have made you into nations and tribes, so you may know one another". God taught Adam the rules by which to live the mortal life on earth where his progeny multiplied and diversified. The principles which God taught Adam remained the same throughout human history. The same principles were the basis of what Moses preached in the Sinai, what Jesus preached in Jerusalem and Bethlehem, and what Muhammad preached in Mecca and Medina. Then how did it become three different faiths at odds with each other? How did they become bitter enemies? That is caused by organized religion which divided humanity and caused people to be at odds with each other. Due to the stakeholders' self-seeking ways, they even became bitter enemies during some historical periods such as the Crusades ordered by the Pope.

Psalm 15 begins with: "Lord, who may enter your sacred tent? Who may dwell on your holy mountain?" It can be appealing, beautiful and universal if the answer is 'anyone and everyone'. Lord God is God of all, and His tent and His mountain are open to all. But would all of them agree to share God's tent and God's Mountain? A cursory look upon God's earth reveals that the children of Adam mostly cannot stand each other; each is engaged in finding fault with the faith of the other, condemn it and look down upon it. Each is adamant that God belongs exclusively to them. Each would be expected to make an exclusive claim to the tent of God and the mountain of God.

Wendell Berry wrote a book based on Matthew 5:9. Title of his book: "Blessed are the Peacemakers: Christ's Teachings of Love, Compassion, and

---

[11] Genesis 2:7.
[12] Genesis 2:22.
[13] Genesis 3:20.

Forgiveness."[14] In that book he writes: "Especially among Christians in positions of wealth and power, the idea of reading the Gospels and keeping Jesus' commandments as stated therein has been replaced by a curious process of logic. According to this process, people first declare themselves to be followers of Christ, and then they assume that whatever they say or do merits the adjective "Christian"".

He mentioned only Christians, but this statement is equally true about, and applicable to every organized religion. One commonly finds a disconnect between what a faith teaches and what the faithful claim to believe and practice. The self-appointed guardians of Islam have given themselves the same right and authority to decide and define what Islam is, and then to insist that everyone should dutifully and obediently follow their assertion.

Reza Shah-Kazemi wrote "My Mercy Encompasses All" based on 'The Koran's Teachings on Compassion, Peace & Love'. Wendell Berry wrote the Foreword. In it he wrote that the followers of Koran and Bible are "divided into two groups: those who appoint themselves as agents of God's anger, and those who understand themselves as called to be agents of divine mercy. As never before, I thought of the unimaginable distance between God's anger and God's love – and of the speed with which Christians sometimes move from God's presumed anger at other people to His presumptive love for themselves."[15] Again, he modestly mentions only Christians, but the statement applies equally to all faiths.

That is the same as what Robert Young in the role of Episcopalian pastor said, "about the way we use words like meanness and intolerance and bigotry but somehow we manage to use them in connection with other people but never with ourselves."

When we reach into the scriptures, we find social harmony commanded very strongly. Qur'an opens with the statement: "Glory to God, the Lord of the universe". That includes everyone and everything, and He is not the Lord of any one group of people. God requires that we believe in him, but parameters of belief are wide. The second chapter begins by defining a believer as the one who believes in the transcendental God, establishes a

---

[14] Blessed Are the Peacemakers, Christ's Teachings About Love, Compassion and Forgiveness, by Wendell Berry (2005)

[15] My Mercy Encompasses All: The Koran's Teachings on Compassion, Peace and Love, by Reza Shah-Kazemi and Wendell Berry | Sep 28, 2007

permanent connection with Him, spends the bounty from God for humanity's benefit, and believes in the current and all the previous revelations, meaning Torah and Gospel and other scriptures. In the second chapter, the believer's domain is further expanded. "Those who believe and those of the Jewish Faith and the Christians and the Sabian; any who believe in God and the Last Day and live their life doing good deeds; shall have their reward with their Lord and on them shall be no fear nor shall they grieve."[16] In this verse Sabian is most probably a catch-all phrase meaning everyone else. That would make the statement apply to everyone. But some Muslim scholars work very hard to search for people in the past somewhere on earth who can be labeled as Sabian. That effort seeks to narrow an all-inclusive message into a message exclusive for a particular group. Such efforts are widespread over all organized religions and the scriptures are made to support them by creative interpretations.

Quran must have anticipated this human tendency; it makes a much stronger statement a little later in the same chapter; "Whoever submits self to God and is engaged in doing good, will have a reward from the Lord, and will have nothing to fear and nothing to grieve."[17] Quran makes further declarations to remove differentiation between communities bearing different faith labels: "The food of the People of the Book is lawful unto you and your food is lawful unto them."[18] Usually, food is a strong dividing element and that is specifically removed here. Jesus summed it up: "Do to others as you would have them do to you."[19] Rabbi Hillel said the same thing.

Jesus talked to everyone, and anyone could come to him. Now only dues paying 'members' can worship in churches built in his name. Christians of Najran came to meet Prophet Muhammad in the mosque. When it was time for their prayer, they wanted to go somewhere to pray. Prophet told them to pray right in the mosque. Now some Muslims would not allow anyone of another faith to pray in the mosque; they even do not want anyone to enter their beloved mosque.

Social harmony among people is ordained by God. It is blocked by humans who build barriers in the name of organized religions.

---

[16] Quran 2:62
[17] Quran 2:112
[18] Quran 5:5
[19] Luke 6:31

I argue from the scriptures, as well as on the philosophical basis, that people within themselves have innate capabilities to chart the course of their lives using these innate capabilities, perhaps supplemented with the guidance of God including via scriptures, without the need for an organized religion to navigate between people and God. This is the course that seems optimal for all those who feel the presence of inner inspiration via the innate capabilities within themselves.

In the following two chapters, I will explore one aspect of this optimal path in some detail, namely the aspect of free will.

# 3. Power and Corruption of Religious Establishments

*Humans desire power for control and domination. Power corrupts and absolute power corrupts absolutely. The greatest amount of power is concentrated in religious and political establishments which use it to control, suffocate and hurt those who gave them the power, but often face no consequences.*

"Over one thousand child victims were identified by our investigation, though the Grand Jury notes that they believed that number was in the thousands." That is what Pennsylvania Attorney General Josh Shapiro said in his graphical description of child sexual abuse by Catholic priests, as reported by Washington Post on August 14, 2018. It was extremely painful to listen to Mr. Shapiro as he went on with the detailed description of one abuse after another, just in Pennsylvania; the total impact is nationwide, even worldwide. The painful agony on the faces of those sitting around him, and listening to him, was so powerfully visible. There were more details in the text of the story written by Michelle Boorstein, Reporter, and Gary Gately. That story was even more painful and more difficult to read. "More than 300 Catholic priests across Pennsylvania sexually abused children over seven decades, protected by a hierarchy of church leaders who covered it up," they wrote. "The investigation," they added, "identified 1,000 children who were victims, but reported that there probably are thousands more."[1]

Writing this here is an agony, which makes one reflect how Josh Shapiro might have felt when he was telling the story and how Michelle Boorstein, Reporter, and Gary Gately felt when writing it.

---

[1] https://www.washingtonpost.com/news/acts-of-faith/wp/2018/08/14/pennsylvania-grand-jury-report-on-sex-abuse-in-catholic-church-will-list-hundreds-of-accused-predator-priests/?utm_term=.09e856da87cf

Michelle Boorstein and Tara Bahrampour later (August 30, 2018) reported in the Acts of Faith section of Washington Post about "Victims of a prominent Orthodox rabbi who spied for years on women in a ritual bath". Bernard "Barry" Freundel "placed a hidden camera in the changing room of a mikvah, a ritual bath Jews use for various purposes, including as part of the conversion process". They reported that in 2015, "Freundel was sentenced to six and a half years in prison after pleading guilty to videotaping 52 women without their knowledge". Victims complained that the community "allowed Freundel to exploit his power over them".[2]

The question bubbling in one's mind is what causes humans to act this way. As discussed in the previous chapter, one possible answer might be found in the declaration by Lord Acton that: "Power tends to corrupt and absolute power corrupts absolutely." Human society has given so much power and so much authority to its religious leaders – be they priests, pastors, rabbis, mullahs or pundits – and to their political leaders – be they presidents, prime ministers or kings – that some of them get intoxicated by that power and use it for selfish purposes, hurting and harming so many in the process and causing untold misery and agony. They do it in the name of the great law givers and preachers – Moses, Jesus, Muhammad, and Buddha – when in fact they are violating and corrupting the teachings of those great men. As Lord Acton added: "There is no worse heresy than that the office sanctifies the holder of it." It is we, the believers, who, with our reverence for our religious leaders, enable them in their excesses. It is we, with our indifference and devil-may-care attitude, who enable our political leaders to corrupt the system for their own personal greed and glory. When we abdicate our responsibility to exercise our constitutional obligation to participate in the decision-making process by exercising our right to vote and abdicate our spiritual obligation to study and understand the principles and commandments of our faith, we have no choice but to suffer the consequences. We hand the leaders – religious as well as political – absolute power. They use it for their own benefit, frequently hurting us in the process. But they get away scot-free, because 'the office sanctifies the holder'.

---

[2]  https://www.washingtonpost.com/news/acts-of-faith/wp/2018/08/28/orthodox-jewish-organizations-reach-14-5-million-settlement-with-victims-of-voyeur-rabbi-barry-freundel/?utm_term=.45217120d1e0

Throughout human history, those who were sanctified by their office have made the rules and forced everyone to follow those rules. There have been very few who dared to challenge those rules, and people have rarely paid attention to what these challengers had to say. The religious establishment has exercised its authority with impunity to suffocate ideas and torture those who dared to present knowledge – no matter how sound – which did not comply with the rules and demands of the religious establishment. It is well known as to what happened to Socrates, Galileo, Spinoza, Ahmad Bin Hanbal, Mansur, and so many others, under the judgment of the religious authority. Religious authority has acquired absolute power which is impossible to challenge. When it has given itself the ultimate power to make the rules with no checks and balances, it ensures its own survival, and the ability to control those under its power. Political power gets the free hand because we abdicate our constitutional obligation to participate and lead, thereby enabling those who rise to power, not to serve but to rule for selfish reasons and for self-gratification.

"Predators in every Diocese weaponized the Catholic Faith and used it as a tool of their abuse," declared Josh Shapiro. That statement applies to every faith. Leadership of every religion weaponizes their faith, perhaps not for the same abuse, which was the subject of this investigation, but definitely to control people by defining their behavior and demanding obedient compliance. They exercise power over people by constantly reminding them of the horrors of hell, to escape which they must obey. Power corrupts and absolute power corrupts absolutely. Religious establishment exercises absolute power, and we acquiesce willingly, to our peril.

Washington Post published a report by Barkha Dutt in May of 2017 (5-5-2017)[3] about a practice among Indian Muslims, known as triple talaq, by which a man grants himself the right to divorce his wife just by repeating the word 'divorce' three times. This practice has the full sanction and support of the Indian Islamic establishment even though it is a total violation of the Quranic commandments on the subject. When the issue came before India's Supreme Court to decide its constitutionality, it was strongly opposed by the self-appointed guardians of Islam in India. Barkha

---

[3] What India's liberals get wrong about women and sharia law: by Barkha Dutt: Washington Post May 5, 2017

Dutt wrote in this article: "The Muslim Personal Law Board, a group of self-declared custodians of Islam, has contested attempts to ban triple talaq, even telling the Supreme Court that it's 'better to divorce a woman than kill her'." The Supreme Court ruled the practice unconstitutional, illegal and void by a 3 to 2 majority. How sad that two justices saw nothing wrong with such a horrible misogynist practice.

Church child abuse, children being snatched at the border and triple talaq are a small sample of the very large number of horrible consequences of the absolute power – be it religious or political – concentrated in a very few hands, some of whom become intoxicated by that power and use it to hurt and abuse. Consequences of our blind obedience to the religious establishment and indifference to the political process leads to drastic consequences. Those of us who are indoctrinated to follow and obey the authority – both religious and political – accept it to be a normal and necessary process, and fault those who dare to question such behavior, labeling them as unpatriotic and sacrilegious trouble makers.

"These are the times that try men's souls", a very famous quote from Thomas Paine. He was talking about the time when our country was struggling for its very identity. We might assume that those times ended with our victory in the Revolutionary War. But such times never end. They continue to try not only men's souls but women's souls too. They try the souls of the believers and shake their faith. The believers in God are forced to wonder why God lets these things happen. Believers have been taught, by the religious establishment, from their infancy, that God judges our every act and is constantly engaged in rewarding our good deeds and punishing our bad deeds. We have been conditioned to fear God's constant and ever-present judgment of everything we do or say, lest we end up in hell. We need our religious leaders, we are indoctrinated to believe, to save us from hell and therefore we must obey them at all times. We wonder why God is allowing many to do all the things that we have been taught not to do; why God is allowing them to do all these horrible things and not stopping them and not punishing them. Then we find that those who taught us what to do and what not to do, are themselves not following those teachings and are horribly violating them. And God did not stop them nor punish them. We see their innocent victims suffering under their horrible acts and find that God is letting them suffer. We find ourselves facing times that try not only our souls but also our faith.

Religion and politics generate very strong emotions leading to strong emotional attachments to the causes. That is free will in action. Those who exercise the power to control, both to benefit and to harm, are often blindly followed by many. Those who follow blindly are also exercising their free will to do so. They might be following blindly because they might not have stopped to assess the consequences of doing so. They might also not have stopped to analyze what they are following, assess its validity, its benefit or harm. Perhaps they should make an attempt to assess and understand what they are required to follow, evaluate its merits, and then decide if to follow or not. That is also the exercise of free will. However, an observation of human behavior shows that most people are not undertaking such an analysis and examination. Not to do it may also be an exercise of free will. Or could that be for them a pre-ordained destiny? It is hard to say.

"Nearly all men can stand adversity, but if you want to test a man's character, give him power." Abraham Lincoln

"My concern is not whether God is on our side; my greatest concern is to be on God's side, for God is always right." Abraham Lincoln

"The will of God prevails. In great contests each party claims to act in accordance with the will of God. Both may be, and one must be wrong. God cannot be for and against the same thing at the same time." Abe Lincoln.

Next chapter will explore Free Will in detail.

# 4. God and Free Will

*The only workable meaning of human free will is the one that derives from fully exercising the reasoning and intellectual faculties. Alternatives based on myriads of scriptural interpretations, and making appeal to various dogmas of organized religion, are neither functionally workable nor do they converge to a meaning that can be agreed upon among the scriptures and their religious interpretations, including the dogmatic ones.*

The Great Battle described in Mahabharat was desired by some and resisted by many. This conversation between Lord Krishna, Queen Draupadi and King Yudhishthir is on that subject.

Draupadi: (who desired the war) War will happen, right? (***Par yeh yudh ho ga, na?***)

Krishna: Even though I do not want it, still, war will happen. (***Main chahta to nahin, phir bhi, yudh to ho ga.***)

Yudhishthir: (who had just entered) If you do not want it, Vasudev, then how can there be war?

Krishna: Did I wish for Draupadi to be disrobed (***vaster haran***), Big Brother. That is the very complication (***kathnai***) that everything in the world (***sansar***) does not happen because I want it to happen. (***Sansar mein sub kuchh mere chahne ke anusar nahin hota.***) Therefore, this war will also happen, because it has been decided by the untied hair (***khule kase***) of Draupadi, it has been decided by the jealousy (***esha***) of Duryodhan, it has been decided by the false desire (***ucha kansha***) of Dhritrashter.

This dialogue is from the epic Mahabharat, a sacred Hindu scripture. According to this epic, and for those Hindus who believe in it, Krishna is

47

God in human incarnation, just as Jesus is God in human form for
Christians. Draupadi had a mysterious origin as she was not born in a
normal way but had emerged from the fire. Even though it is not stated
openly, there is a subtle implication that she might be something more than
human. Thus, she might have known that Krishna was God, a fact which
was not known to anyone else, with the very possible exception of Ganga-
puttar Bhisham. The way Yudhishthir asks that question, there appears to
be a latent and implicit hint that he might have had some idea as to who
Krishna was.

It is extraordinary that Krishna, who is supposed to be God incarnate,
would declare that not everything in the world happens according to what
God wants. This idea of things happening and events taking place without
God wanting them or ordering them to happen, is at variance from, or even
contradictory to, the belief in an all-powerful, all seeing and all-knowing
God, without whose express permission and command nothing can ever
happen. All believers are taught by their religious authority that nothing
happens on earth or anywhere else in the universe without God's
permission and command. Normal and positive happenings are explained as
the Grace of God. Negative happenings, no matter how tragic and horrible,
are explained as the punishment caused by the anger of God against human
misconduct. That thought process becomes difficult – even impossible – to
comprehend when things happen without any possible explanations or any
visible human misconduct on the part of the victims who suffer terribly.

Faithful of all faiths hold that there is a Divine Plan which has been in
place since the beginning of time and anything that ever happens is in strict
compliance with that Divine Plan. It is a common Christian belief that
nothing can happen without God's permission. Christians believe in Devil
who is held to be responsible for causing bad things to happen, but they
also believe that even Devil has to seek God's permission to do his bad
deeds; a notion perhaps on the basis of Job 1:12. When Satan said to God
that Job would turn against Him if the Divine blessings were denied him,
God gave Satan permission with restrictions. "Very well, then, everything he
has is in your power, but on the man himself, do not lay a finger."

Muslims also take the same position that even a leaf on a tree cannot
move without the express permission of God. For this firmly held opinion,
some may attempt to find justification and evidence in the Quran. For
example, Quran 3:26: "SAY: 'O God, Lord of all dominion! You grant

dominion unto whom You will and take away dominion from whom You will; and You exalt whom You will and abase whom You will. In Your hand is all good. Verily, You have the power to will anything."

Muslims also believe in Devil and blame him for causing all the troubles and confusions, but they also declare that he is doing it with the express permission of God, who can stop him any time if He so chooses.

Many Hindus would declare that it is mentioned in the scriptures that Krishna is the all-doer and not a blade of grass moves without His will, notwithstanding Krishna's own assertion that not everything happens because He wants it to or has commanded it to.

Hindus also believe in Free Will for humans but hold that the free will is subject to and is constrained by Karma, a concept which has gained acceptance and popularity in the West. But Karma is very hard to define and almost impossible to understand. About its meanings or importance there is no agreement among various schools of Hinduism and Buddhism; in fact, there is a wide disagreement, and some do not accept it at all.

Humans have a great capacity to rationalize and find 'reasonable' explanations for tragically horrible happenings; they can even find great benefits in those tragedies. Of course, those who claim to find such great benefits are the ones who were not trapped by the tragedy, were not victimized by it, watched it or heard about it from a safe distance and therefore did not suffer any misery caused by the tragedy. They are separated from the tragic events by distance or by time. In the comfort of their safe and secure space, far from the happenings which cause many to suffer, such wise men and women rationalize to find great benefits resulting from horrible events at a great distance from them or far in the past.

Two thousand years after Saint Paul suffered in prison, someone would be able to rationalize that God inflicted that misery on Paul to make the jailer a believer, as if God was unable to do it without making Paul suffer. God caused Jesus to suffer on the cross so he could be resurrected, because God – the omnipotent – was not capable of creating the same result without making His Son go through the unspeakable agony of crucifixion. A rationalizing person would find great good in every misery and agony which the rationalizer did not suffer.

Muslims always discover Divine Purpose – often expressed by the Arabic word *Muslehat* – in every bad thing which happens to someone else.

Hindus and Buddhists chart such sufferings out to the illusive concept of Karma.

Krishna points to a way for a better understanding of events, both good and bad, by declaring that not everything happens in the world because God wants it to happen, or He makes it to happen. In the above dialogue, Krishna explains that the war will happen despite him not wanting it, because the war has actually been decided by human actions. There is a strong, all encompassing, causality at work.

How and why do things happen then? Is the answer in the scriptures?

Scriptures express complex principles in allegories and metaphors. They do not always necessarily mean what they appear to be saying by their literal meanings. Most of the time they require – in fact demand – some interpretation of the literal expressions. That is where all the problems arise. Since multiple interpretations are always possible, there develop many points of view attached to various different interpretations. As long as it is recognized by all the people that different interpretations may lead to different outlooks for the same principles, and all agree to respect the other's point of view, there would be no problem. But that is the very thing that just about always fails to happen. Every individual and every group of individuals become so attached to their own interpretation of the various concepts expressed allegorically and metaphorically, that they insist that only 'their' interpretation is correct while all others are wrong.

If they stop at that point, more complex problems could still be avoided; but they do not stop there. They adamantly demand that everyone else must abandon all the 'wrong' interpretations and understandings and dutifully adopt 'their' 'correct' interpretation. When there are so many 'correct' interpretations of the same principles, each claiming to be 'the only correct interpretation' and 'the exclusive ultimate truth', conflict is obvious and unavoidable.

A careful reading of the scriptures would make it obvious that the scriptures do not say what the self-appointed guardians of faith claim and declare to be their meanings. Scriptures elaborate the power of God and His unlimited ability to control everything in the universe which is after all His creation and so is the system and the natural plan which operate and sustain the universe. It does not mean that God is actually controlling everything all the time like a puppeteer controls the puppets. Some people might desire for God to control everything on a moment-by-moment basis, and some may firmly believe that he is doing it, but that does not mean that God actually does it.

The Biblical verses on this topic indicate His power but do not imply that He does or even wants to control every single event, no matter how large or how small. "Mortals make elaborate plans, but God has the last word"[1]; it points to the infinite power of God compared to infinitesimal human ability. When it is written that "the earth is the Lord's, and everything in it, the world, and all who live in it"[2], it states an obvious truth which does not necessarily lead to the conclusion that He is engaged in controlling every event. God states the same obvious truth in the statement "Everything under heaven belongs to me"[3]; or when Job acknowledged the power of God by saying "I know that you can do all things; no purpose of yours can be thwarted"[4]. He can definitely do all things if He chooses to, which He may or may not.

When Pilate told Jesus that he had the power to free him or to crucify him, Jesus pointed to the obvious truth; "You would have no power over me if it were not given to you from above".[5]

The fact that Jesus was crucified would show that God watches over everything but allows humans to exercise their free will in any way they choose. This would appear to be a well-reasoned position.

We have the option to choose our God-given gift of reasoning and intellectual power, or to shut up the reasoning and intellectual faculties to uncritically fall back on dogma. It would seem prudent to take a reasonable approach by offering thanks to God for having blessed us with our reasoning and intellectual faculties, as well as our conscience that helps us discriminate between right and wrong.

When Qur'an tells the believers to place their trust in God by saying "Never can anything befall us save what God has decreed!"[6] it is a statement and act of faith on the part of the humans and not a declaration of God's constant and on-going management of events. The same statement is repeated in a more general application as "No Calamity can ever befall the

----

[1] Proverbs 16:1.
[2] Psalm 24:1.
[3] Job 41:11.
[4] Job 42:1-2.
[5] John 19:11.
[6] Quran 9:51.

earth, and neither your own selves, unless it be [laid down] in our decree before we bring it into being".[7] The Arabic word is '*kitab*'. The literal meaning of '*kitab*' is 'book', but it has been used in the Qur'an with different meanings in various places. Here, Asad translates it as 'decree', but it could easily be rendered as 'plan'. Later discussion, here, would deal with it as 'plan of the universe' as established by God.

Karma is used by some to explain events, both good and bad. But what is Karma? The word could mean action, work or deed. The Karma Doctrine deals with the spiritual principle of cause and effect; its primary theme is the principle of causality. Karma Doctrine postulates the cycle of death and rebirth (samsara). Intent and action have consequences which could manifest in this life or a future life. This principle is stated in many of the scriptural authorities such as: "As a man himself sows, so he himself reaps."[8] Thus, Karma is the sum of the fruits, both good and bad, of a person's actions in the present and previous states of existence, which decide that person's fate in future existences.

It would appear that Karma deals with individuals, their intentions and actions and the consequences of their actions. This Doctrine does not appear to explain events which impact large sections of the populations, unless the Doctrine is extended to be applied to actions of groups of people and their consequences. There does not appear to be any evidence of such an extension. Even in its application to individual actions and consequences, there does not seem to be a universal agreement on either the precise meaning of the concept or the mode of its application. There are many different definitions of karma, ranging from rigidly deterministic to those which allow for the exercise of free will. Various schools of Hinduism and Buddhism address the internal inconsistencies, implications and issues of the karma doctrine by taking positions on a wide spectrum, ranging from holding karma and rebirth as central, to it being not important at all. Many do not think it can explain evil, inequality and other observable facts about society. Karma might be an acceptable explanation for the frequently recurring events that cause human misery for those who hold it as the central doctrine, but it does not have universal acceptance or mode of application.

---

[7] Quran 57:22.
[8] Mahabharata, xii. 291.22.

That brings us back to what Krishna declared. "Not everything in the world happens according to what I want." ***Sansar main sub kuchh mere chahne ke anusar nahin hota.*** Leaders of every faith hold that God is all powerful and controls everything in the universe on an ongoing basis. They view God as personal God who is engaged in the progress of human life every minute. There is no question that God is all powerful; He created the universe and established a system and a plan for its operation. He established the laws of nature according to which the universe is constantly evolving and growing. He created life including human life and gave all creatures, including humans, the knowledge and ability with which to control their mortal life. He also gave humans free will to use their knowledge and their abilities as they please and deem best.

Having given them free will, He has left them alone to live in the universe which operates under the built-in laws of nature. Whether the humans exist for one mortal life or go through a cycle of death and rebirth, which may or may not ultimately result in after life, in the life on this earth – one life or many – they are free to live as they please. God may judge them in the afterlife – evaluate their performance on earth – to decide what kind of life they have earned in the hereafter. That life in the hereafter is not necessarily a life of eternal misery or eternal bliss – as many preachers claim – but a life with varying levels of comfort, from which people may be able to advance, up or down. This would seem to be a reasonable path for us because the alternative based on dogma under the command of the human religious authority is prone to a wide range of suffocating commands and constraints based on dogmas. We need to appreciate that the will of a person becomes a free-will only after God has blessed it by setting it free from dogmatic constraints.

Human activity and conduct – individual and collective – are just one force among the forces in the universe. There are many more. All these forces are working to interact with each other according to the plan and system established by the creator of the universe. It is this plan that is referred to as the Kitab in the Qur'an, God's last word mentioned in the Bible, and the Will of Krishna mentioned in the Hindu Tradition.

There are a multitude of forces in nature, each in possession of its own unique qualities and characteristics and each governed by its own designated natural laws. Winds blow at various speeds from very slow to tremendously fast and furious. Rivers flow at various levels with multiple speeds, causing erosion and frequently overflowing to cause floods. Heat and cold create different weather and climate conditions, which can sometimes be very comfortable but very severe at other times. Oceans are vast and deep and respond to climate conditions to cause tsunamis and hurricanes. The core of the earth is always actively boiling and agitating, often causing earthquakes. Fire is a highly beneficial agent for human existence but can sometimes get out of control and cause havoc. There are many more natural forces.

Beside these natural forces, there is human activity. In everything the humans do maybe some good for all, but at least for some a great harm. Even those activities which are undertaken for the good of humanity may have harmful side effects which may or may not be known at the time. Freon was considered to be a great and admirable product and used extensively for a long time until its harmful contribution to ozone depletion was discovered. That is only one example of a product created by humans for human benefit with a negative impact on nature. Climate change or global warming is now of major concern as it is understood to be caused by a multitude of human activities. Those are just the side effects of the beneficial human activities. Then there are deliberate human activities which are driven by greed, ego and desire to grab power. Such activities lead to human misery deliberately caused by humans. The tragedy of the two world wars, Holocaust in Germany during the 1940's and tragedy of Punjab in 1947 are just some of the examples. All such things are caused by humans in the exercise of their free-will with the utilization of their God-given intellect to think and plan.

Nature and Humans combine to create many results, some beneficial and some harmful. Humans usually take credit for the beneficial results of their actions but assign the responsibility for harmful results to God. It is not so. God just watches His system to operate according to the rules which He has built into that system. God is not causing these things to happen nor is He planning to interfere to redirect the operation of the natural laws and human activity, either to help or to harm.

So how do we understand and explain natural disasters? And what about man's inhumanity to man? Nepal and Bihar earthquakes of 1934 killed up to 12,000 people and destroyed entire cities. San Francisco earthquake of 1906 killed 3,000 people and destroyed the city. Chicago Fire of 1871 burned for three days, killed up to 300 people, destroyed roughly 3.3 square miles of the city, and left more than 100,000 residents homeless. Kashmir

Earthquake of 2005 devastated Kashmir and northwestern Pakistan, was felt in Afghanistan, Tajikistan, India and China. It killed upward of 100,000 people – including 19,000 children plus 250,000 farm animals, both of whom are supposed to be innocent – and rendered over 3.5 million people homeless. The Holocaust of the 1940's resulted in the systematic murder by Nazi Germany of six million people, a devastating genocide of Jews, the Roma, the "incurably sick", Poles, other Slavic groups, Soviet citizens and prisoners of war, homosexuals, Jehovah's Witnesses, black people, and political opponents. In 1947, the Punjab experienced a holocaust of its own in which between one and two million people were killed and between 15 and 20 million were made homeless, in a senseless communal bloodbath. The gulf coast of America, the Caribbean Islands and the surrounding areas are devastated by hurricanes and tsunamis year after year. In the year 2017, several of them – 10 hurricanes in 10 weeks – came with a vengeance, one after the other, causing death and destruction in large magnitude. California Fires – an ongoing phenomenon year after year – reduced entire communities to ash in 2017. These are only a few examples of the countless natural disasters and man-made human tragedies over thousands of years of human existence.

It is not possible to explain all of these and infinitely many more tragic events by Karma or simply as anger of God on human misconduct. Such perplexities have led some to the paradox of free will, which would postulate that omniscience and free will are incompatible and that any conception of God that incorporates both properties is therefore inconceivable. That is a complex dilemma for which a solution is urgently needed but would appear to be almost impossible to obtain.

Free will is as difficult a concept as is karma. It is very hard to fully grasp it. There is a vast difference of opinion on its precise meanings as well as its proper application.

رب اک گھنجلدار بجھارت    رب اک گورکہ دھندا
اس گھنجل نون کھوجن لگیا    کافر ہو جاے بندا

*God is a complex puzzle, a mysterious conundrum.*
*Anyone attempting to solve the puzzle may lose his faith.*

The concept of free will is so complicated and confusing that someone attempting to understand, grasp, untangle it may end up first losing his/her mind and finally his/her faith. Such attempts create self-doubt among those who undertake them. Self-doubt is not necessarily bad, because it motivates thinking and inquiry which may lead to great progress. But it is troubling, nevertheless. Blessed are those with the gift of a strong faith. These two groups look at free will very differently. There is a big debate about God's grant of free will to humans. Are humans free to exercise their God given abilities to do whatever they want whichever way they want without any interference or obstruction from anyone, not even God? Or does the all-powerful God have complete control on each and every aspect of human life? That debate constantly rages not only between people – individuals or groups – but it often rages within the mind of the same person. This debate is so debilitating that the person struggling with it, unable to find a satisfactory solution, may find oneself completely lost, and driven to rebel against the commonly accepted norms and to reject them outright. Such persons may either become rebels against the status quo or get burned in the fire of their anger. Or such persons may turn their anger into positive energy to make tremendous contributions to human knowledge and progress, as so many have done.

The debate between free will and divine control needs to be resolved. Divine Will and Power are undeniable realities for all believing people. Those who choose not to believe might question this statement, but that is fine; that is their God-given right.

For the believing people, scriptures provide substantive guidance. But do the believing people read the scriptures for their meanings to seek wisdom and guidance, or do they read them only for their sound, strictly in search of the elusive goal of salvation in the hereafter? Evidence points to the latter approach. That approach may lead some to complain that God should take at least some responsibility for the bad outcomes, because He is supposed to be all knowing. That sentiment could have some merit, or it could simply be a way to shirk the personal responsibility demanded by the grant of free will.

Scriptures are supposed to be the rule books of guidance on how to live this mortal life. They are supposed to lead the believers to an understanding by way of reason. Reason must be the foundation of faith. Reason provides strength to belief. Reason takes the believer beyond the dogma and provides freedom from the rituals. Reason builds a life of morality and justice with a deep abiding respect for fellow humans. Reason guides the believer to a proper understanding of God as the creator, the sustainer, the granter of free will and the ultimate Judge after His creatures have completed their sojourn on this earth – one or many. The granter of free will has left His creatures to their own doing during their mortal life. He does not interfere in their affairs and activities, nor does He attempt to control or redirect them. However, in the hereafter – if there is a hereafter – He will Judge His creatures and reward them according to their performance on earth in His Final Judgment.

Man's inhumanity to man is strictly the human doing. It can be prevented if humans apply reason in understanding and adopting the moral code of the Divine Plan which is contained in every available scripture. Natural disasters are not caused by humans even though they may unwittingly contribute to them. They are caused by the immense powers of nature operating under their designated plan. Some may hope and want God to control the Nature, but that would be a personal God constantly engaged in controlling His creation. He has placed his creation in place, instituted a definite plan for its operation, and it is operating according to that plan. It is very possible that He wants Humans to have better control on the working of the Nature. With advanced knowledge and technology, humans can and should acquire the ability to control the elements of Nature to some extent, even if they cannot be fully controlled.

Krishna suggests a solution and that solution is logical and is compatible with observed phenomena and the essence of reason. Thomas Paine in Age of Reason stated that "the Word of God cannot exist in any written or human language". He declared: "The Word of God is the Creation We Behold: And it is in this word, which no human invention can counterfeit or alter, that God speaks universally to man".[9] Qur'an makes the same declaration. The opponents of the message of the Qur'an, who were constantly demanding a proof of the existence of God, were told to look for the signs of God in the creation around them and within themselves.[10] According to Thomas Paine, the choicest gift of God to man is the Gift of Reason. Somehow, we have relegated reason to obscurity and adopted dogma as our guide.

---

[9] The Age of Reason: Thomas Paine, 1807, Chapter 9, page 27.
[10] Quran 45:3-5, 51:20-21, 6:75, 28:77.

We need to abandon dogma and return to a full utilization of reason in order to obtain maximum benefit. This free will is free from all external interference; God has set it free of even His own interference, which act has blessed the human will to become a free will. The only well-reasoned and non-dogmatic approach is that God allows the human free will to operate unstinted.

The next chapter explores the Refugee Experience.

# 5. *Surviving Refugee Trauma*

*There are cases of human suffering caused by Natural forces and those caused by the inhumanity of man towards man. Many of the victims are innocent. It is legitimate to enquire how God's mercy, love, and justice operate. God has blessed man with an unstinted free will. When all else is lost, the gift of free will endures and keeps alive a ray of hope.*

The journey in search of meaning continues. The previous chapters explored the creative power of God, in whom many believe but some may not. The belief in God leads to religion which is a set of principles to guide human life. Humans have free will, which empowers them to decide how to live their life. Free will offers the opportunity to create a wholesome environment for human existence with the application of adopted principles and ideals. But it also provides an opportunity for the powerful to control and subjugate the weak. God does not limit or restrain the exercise of free will by anyone. But humans do, who frequently invoke God in doing it. There are many forces which are actively engaged in controlling human behavior and suffocating human activity. Perhaps the most powerful such force is the organized religion. And there are others, such as national pride, racial and cultural superiority, military power, and so on. Any of these forces or a combination of some or all of them can produce disastrous results for a multitude of people, ranging from suffocating subjugation to forced expulsion from their homes and regions. The refugee phenomenon is a direct result of the exercise of free will by the powerful in the name of religion, race, culture or national identity, to inflict misery on the weak. The victims can cling to the promise of God's gift of free love and care, to endure and keep alive a ray of hope.

This chapter is devoted to a discussion of the refugee experience.

Among many forces which may cause people to become refugees, one is nature. Nature sustains us; that is why we call it Mother Nature. But Mother

Nature can sometime be very cruel. It causes floods, hurricanes, tsunamis, earthquakes and California fires. It is hard to say if Nature does this deliberately to hurt people or it is just doing what is normal and people happen to be in the way; perceived as people happening to be at the wrong place at the wrong time. The mercy of God and the all-encompassing love of God is supposed to be ever present, though people suffering through these situations seldom are the recipients of such mercy and such love in their hour of need. They cannot be blamed for doubting if that mercy is real.

But when it comes to man's inhumanity to man, there is no doubt; it is deliberate. It began when Cain killed Abel. And it never stopped. Slavery was a deliberate human act. Apartheid in many places is a deliberate human act. Holocaust was a deliberate act of Nazi Germany who systematically murdered at least six million people, including Jews, the Roma (Gypsies), the "incurably sick", Poles, other Slavic groups, Soviet citizens and prisoners of war, homosexuals, Jehovah's Witnesses, black people, and political opponents. We frequently hear about survivors of that horrible, horrible tragedy, which we should never forget. We can hope that anything like that should never happen again. But unfortunately, it does happen, again and again, and continues to happen. Many such horrible acts of man's inhumanity to man, which occurred in the past, continue to cause suffering to many, up to our times and maybe beyond our times.

Native Americans have been confined to what the civilized world calls Reservations and they continue to linger in those confinements. It happened in Rwanda, in Bosnia, in Darfur, and in various Apartheid regimes. It continues to happen in what many call the Holy Land, where those driven from their homes have lived in refugee camps for over three generations, and may have to live for who knows how many more generations. People are being forced by lawlessness and violence in their homelands in many parts of the world, including India and Burma. Rohyngas in Burma are being wiped out from human memory and world is watching with a total indifference. Endless conflicts and violence in the Levant are causing a flood of refugees seeking shelter in Europe and North America, while the safe havens are being shut in their faces. Powerful nations occupy and exploit those who are not able to defend themselves. Occupiers control the conversation, present themselves as the benefactors, and demand that the occupied people be grateful for their benevolence, should willingly accept their subjugation and openly express their gratitude. The occupied people linger under the oppressive rule of the occupiers. The few who escape become refugees. If the refugees manage to reach a safe haven which has not yet been shut in their face, an impression is created that these refugees have made it to success; that is a euphemism.

In such situations the victims are left holding the bag of helplessness and desperation – a feeling of desertedness in a place devoid of compassion and justice. One might recall the last words of Christ: "Oh my God why have you forsaken me!"

Analysis shows that we can still rejoice, for God so loved mankind that He gave each one a free will. When the victims are stripped to their bare skin, they still are not stripped of their free will, and they still can hope. Human free will helps people dream for better days even under such dire circumstances.

I was once a refugee. I was 7 years old when India and Pakistan became independent countries in 1947. My state of Punjab was divided between India and Pakistan, and we were in the Indian part. We did not care; India or Pakistan, this was our home and that is where we were going to live. Things were fairly normal in our area and people of all faiths got along very well. But then something happened that changed everything. The largest Muslim village in our region was attacked. The village was set on fire and a large number of people were killed. The Muslims of the area witnessed that tragic incidence with horror. They panicked. We could be next. To escape the danger, we fled in search of a safe place to hide, fully expecting to return when danger passed. The danger never passed, and we never returned. We continued on our journey through hell that took four months.

We had to cross a big river which had no bridge, we were robbed by the Indian Army, and we had to spend two months in a refugee camp. After a four-month journey through hell we reached Pakistan expecting a warm welcome but received none. Instead, the local people, in every area we passed, looked down upon us as the wretch of the earth even though we never asked anybody for anything. Nobody – neither common people nor officials of Pakistan Government – enquired about our condition and nobody ever offered any help. They did not even talk to us. They were contemptuous of our presence and just did not want us around.

All through the journey of four miserable months, we lived on God's bare earth, under God's open sky, exposed to all the elements of nature; hot summer sun and heavy rains. When the river flooded and water was everywhere, we had to live in knee deep water for days. Then came the Cholera Epidemic which killed a lot of people. And every day, we heard stories about people being killed by armed men. Many died of starvation. Punjab suffered a senseless communal bloodbath which made between 15 and 20 million people homeless refugees and left a couple of million dead. In Pakistan, smallpox epidemic broke out to cause many more deaths. This happened right after the Holocaust in Germany and caused just as much misery and suffering.

One thing about the Punjab tragedy; it was happening on both sides of the border. Those forced to flee were leaving behind their empty houses and vacant properties which were then occupied by those coming in. That helped us to settle down and regain stability within the next few years.

Refugees rarely find such an opportunity. They remain refugees for a very long time, even for generations. I do not know if those of Bosnia-Rwanda-Darfur have found permanent homes by now - as we in Punjab did - but those of Holy Land continue to live in refugee camps to this day. Many Christians and Muslims continue to flee the mainland and the occupied territories to seek refuge in USA and many other countries. And those under oppression also endure for a long time, as we the Indians did under British colonial rule.

It is rare for oppressed people to escape from oppression and become free. But it can happen. There is a story in the Bible, in the Book of Judges, Chapter 18, about the House of Dan who had not been able to secure the possession of their inheritance and "the Amorites forced them back into the hill country and would not let them come down into the plains." They sent a search party to find a land which they could possess. The search party found a place called "Laish, where they noticed the people living carefree lives". These people were "wealthy because their land was very fertile". The search party also noticed that the people "had no allies nearby". When they returned from the expedition, they told the House of Dan; "Come on, let's attack them! We have seen the land, and it is very good". They advised the House of Dan; "Don't hesitate to go there and take it over. When you get there, you will find an unsuspecting people and a spacious land that God has put into your hands". The House of Dan sent six hundred men, "armed for battle", to possess that land. They went "to Laish, against a people at peace and secure. They attacked them with the sword and burned down their city. There was no one to rescue them because they lived a long way from Sidon and had no relationship with anyone else." The House of Dan rebuilt the city for themselves. "They named it Dan after their ancestor Dan, who was born to Israel – though the city used to be called Laish."

The idea of peaceful co-existence with the people of Laish did not even occur to the House of Dan, even though they were aware that the land was spacious and fertile, so that it could accommodate them both. That idea of co-existence almost never occurs to humans. They almost never want to share anything with anyone else, definitely not land; they want to possess it exclusively. In rare incidences, the oppressed people may be able to gain freedom from their oppressors, with or without outside help, and then find people weaker than themselves to overpower and occupy, as did the House of Dan. One might expect that those who have endured oppression would know the pain of oppression and therefore would not do to others what was done to them, as Rabbi Hillel is supposed to have said not to do to others what is hateful to you. One would be wrong. The story of the House of Dan negates that expectation. There are modern examples of that phenomenon. These examples clearly demonstrate that those who remember their own pain and would demand that no one should forget it, would not hesitate for a moment to inflict the same pain on others with the misfortune of being weaker than them.

Some noble sounding sentiments are often heard about all humans deserving freedom, respect, and dignity. But those making such noble statements are widely outnumbered by those who are actively at work to deny people such freedom, respect and dignity. I know both sides from personal experience and knowledge. I was born an Indian, in a land occupied by a foreign power. Now I am a citizen of America which occupies many foreign lands. I do not feel good about this or that. I am troubled by both. But I am unable to do anything about it. It is this interaction between the powerful and the weak that oppresses people and forces some of them to become refugees.

To paraphrase the Flying Dutchman, you with the gift of freedom, secure in your home, in possession of your dignity, citizen of a country you can call your own, pity the refugees, who are now homeless and country-less, but were once secure in their homes like yourself, were proud citizens of a country they could call their own like yourself, were once respected members of their cherished community leading a happy and dignified life.

Their community has been destroyed, their homes have been taken away, and they have been forced out of their country. That home, that country, and that community have now become a distant and obscure memory. They were once independent and able to help others but have now become totally dependent on the mercy of strangers, now helplessly looking for help.

I know how it feels. I still have vivid memories of how people looked down upon us, and how they made us feel ashamed of our condition. The shame and humiliation of that experience; I can still feel. The memory still haunts me.

The discussion in the next chapter presents how the exercise of 'free will' generated varying results for the children of Abraham.

# 6. *Legacy of Patriarch Abraham: Is there Hope for Change?*

*I explore how the legacy of Abraham evolved, took different directions, but each change failed to embrace openness and universality. At each turn it embraced group allegiance, exclusiveness, close mindedness that rejected the challenges of reform, a sense of self-righteousness, and competitive animosity among groups. Visionaries like Abraham, Moses, Jesus, and Mohammad stood for openness for change, inclusiveness to embrace all universal truths and the collective humanity. We pledge allegiance to these visionaries, but not to their vision.*

Growing up in Pakistan, surrounded by people who were all Muslim, I developed a sense that Islam was not only the best faith but the only true faith. Accompanied with that sense was an implicit assumption that the fact of Islam being the best and the only true faith was universally accepted. After all, Abraham proclaimed the faith in God and laid out the foundation of a structure of rules and regulations by which the humans must live. Moses gave that structure a more elaborate, though oral, framework. The oral tradition was kept alive for hundreds of years and was finally reduced to writing after Babylon. Jesus continued the process of further refining and expanding that structure. Mohammad completed the process by finalizing that structure into a comprehensive written code for humans by which to live their mortal life.

To me that process of reasoning and using free will to work things out made a lot of sense and I assumed that it would make the same degree of sense to everyone else.

*How wrong I was!*

In time I was to discover that things are not that simple or that logical when it comes to the human race. The original free will is tamed, shaped, and reshaped continually under various cultural forces and power regimes. The results of exercising it can be surprising or even shocking. Free will is shaped under human traits and human conditions.

One human trait is that they do not like change. Humans are also very possessive; they do not want to share with others what they might consider to be a good thing. Humans use the free will to define and frame things and ideas in their own particular mode. Even a slight variation in the description of their ideas and positions would be vigorously opposed; anyone trying to restate their ideas would be strongly condemned and demonized.

Those who accepted God and the Message of God as formulated by Moses simply refused to share it with anyone else; the Israelites claimed its exclusive ownership. They would not allow any outsider to enter their ranks or share their message.[1] They would not allow any insider to challenge the established principles and practices. Any insider who dared to question the establishment faced severe penalty.

Jesus was an insider who challenged the establishment and ended up paying a very heavy price. Nevertheless, he succeeded in initiating a reform movement, which later became Christianity.

That movement struggled and suffered for a few hundred years but finally became viable and began to grow with the help of a Roman Emperor who adopted the new faith. In time Christianity would become a dominant force in the world, just as the Jewish establishment it grew out of, was once dominant in its own world, earlier. In due time, the Christian challengers had become the establishment.

Remembering that their leader had shown the error of a rigid establishment and challenged to reform it to make it inclusive for all, for the purpose of creating a universal community, one would have expected the Christians to be the promoters of an open and inclusive society. One would be wrong. Somehow that does not seem to be compatible with human

---

[1] Why do people possess such intense desire to control the life and the destiny of others? Why do people insist on denying to others the very same things that they so passionately want for themselves?

nature. Inclusiveness and openness seem to offend human sensibilities, whereas exclusivity seems to thrive. It would seem that free will works very differently when exercised collectively together by a group indoctrinated by a strong dogma.

Soon after the Christians emerged from being persecuted for their faith, and began to acquire power with Imperial help, they became as rigid in their establishment as those whom they had challenged; may be even more so. They did not become open, inclusive, and universal. That is the manifestation of free will in a mob configuration.

In time, another reformer would rise and once again proclaim the message of an inclusive and open society for the entire humanity. His message came to be called Islam. His followers would take the message of Islam to the world with the zeal of new converts and reformers and would make a major contribution to human civilization for hundreds of years. Just like their predecessors – the Christians – these reformers, the Muslims, would also build a powerful ecumenical organization that would dominate the world for almost a thousand years. In time, they also would transform into a rigid establishment, proclaiming themselves to be the exclusive owners of the ultimate truth.

More importantly, the Muslims would find themselves in conflict with the Christians from the very start. That conflict would never end.

An idea is a powerful force. It penetrates human minds and spreads through the word of mouth. In order to become dominant, an idea needs the support of a powerful military force led by capable military leaders. The Abrahamic doctrine lingered in the lands of Canaan and Egypt all through the lives of Abraham, Ismail, Isaac, Jacob and Joseph but did not become a dominant enterprise. Joseph rose to great power in Egypt, but the fortunes of his people became dismal soon after him. It was only under Moses, after the Exodus, that the Hebrews began to achieve success. The secret of that success was the great fighting force, numbered above 600,000 by the Torah, which Moses assembled and trained during forty years in the Wilderness. It was this great fighting force that, under great generals starting with Joshua, conquered the land of Canaan over the next 250 years. They lost their dominance when they became militarily weak. They lost out to those with superior military power.

The doctrine of Jesus was accepted by many, first in the land of Canaan, renamed Palestine by Hadrian in 138, and then in Europe, concentrated in and around Rome. The followers of Christ were devout believers, willing to suffer any hardship for their faith, even death. And hardship they actually suffered for over 300 years at the hands of those who held power. They were persecuted mercilessly, until the Roman Emperor Constantine decided to support the faith by joining it. Then the mighty Roman Empire transformed its role from the persecutors to the protectors of Christianity. Gradually, just about all Roman citizens would become Christians, the Roman Empire would become the Holy Christian Roman Empire, and the Roman armies would become the Armies of Christ. There is no suggestion here that anybody was forced to accept Christianity. However, the faith of those in power acquires special attraction to those living under that power. Power promotes imitation. People are naturally inclined to be like those who hold power, so they would tend to adopt the faith, the culture and the way of life of those in power. Power helps the growth of faith and culture. After Constantine, Rome, which was already powerful, became Christian. That faith was carried to the outer reaches of the Roman power.

The great achievement of the founder of Islam was that he was able to establish in his lifetime not only a large faith community but also a political system of government supported by a powerful military. That political system managed and oversaw the advances made by its military that took orders from the civilian authority. Initially, Arabs were not interested in promoting their new faith to non-Arabs. As the Jews had insisted before them that the faith preached by Moses was exclusively for the Hebrews, by then defined as those born of Jacob, Arabs now similarly insisted that the new faith of Islam was exclusively for the Arabs. However, the Muslim Arabs became very powerful very quickly. The people under their influence might have been impressed – or not – by their behavior and attitude, but they were definitely impressed by their power. These people wanted to be like them and therefore they wanted to join their faith and adopt their culture. But the Arabs resisted the expansion of Islam initially by discouraging others from joining their faith. Karen Armstrong has stated that "until the middle of the eighth century, conversion was not encouraged".[2] That would cover the entire period of Umayyad rule. It is easy to accept that the Umayyad rulers would subscribe to such a belief that Islam belongs exclusively to Arabs. Such thinking is compatible with their

---

[2] Karen Armstrong: Islam, A Short History, page 30

outlook and character. However, the force of Arab power and influence over an increasing part of the world would, sooner and later, overcome such thinking, because a large number of people in new areas under their control would desire to join the powerful by adopting their faith and culture.

That is exactly what happened. The conversion process was openly supported by the next dynasty, the Abbasi.

Those claiming to be the successors to the heritage of Abraham would be divided into three separately distinguished groups. The group formed under Moses, and claiming to be the direct descendants of Jacob, would continue to claim the exclusive ownership of the Lord, God of Israel, and His message. They would reject all challengers and all reformers. Those who followed an insider's challenge to the Jewish establishment, elevated the challenger to the level of God, proclaimed him to be the ultimate Savior, and declared that anyone not accepting him as God and Savior and the only Begotten Son of God, is condemned to hell. Rejecting the Jewish claim to the ownership of the ultimate truth, the Christians challengers declared that their leader had superseded all previous messages and all previous claims and therefore they proclaimed themselves to be now the exclusive owners of the ultimate truth.

Those who followed the outside reformer made a half-hearted attempt to reach out to the two older groups and, having failed to come to a mutual understanding, became as rigid in their own establishment under Islam as their predecessors. Confident that the historical process makes it clear that the ultimate truth, filtered through the efforts of the two previous groups and improved to perfection by their leader, is now in their absolute and exclusive ownership, the Muslims firmly planted themselves on the seat of power.

Each claimed allegiance to Abraham, each claimed to be the inheritor of the Legacy of Abraham, and through their allegiance to and inheritance from Abraham, each made the exclusive claim to the Throne of Abraham. Each group has continued to claim exclusive ownership of the ultimate truth, to the complete exclusion of all those others who do not come into their fold under their strict terms and in total submission to their demands.

The originators, the Jews, who lost their prominence and dominance a long time ago, remained in a position of subordination to others, primarily to the Christians, but never accepted the idea of joining an all-inclusive, open human society. They remained in a conflict, which by and large was not of their own making, was externally imposed on them, and over which they practically had no control.

The Christians lingered under subjugation of others for a few hundred years, during which they suffered immensely. But they finally overcame their persecutors and oppressors with Imperial help, converted their oppressors to their own ranks, and with their help rose to power to become dominant in Europe and Near East. That is when the real troubles of the Jews began and continued for a better part of two millennia. The Muslims rose to power very fast, and exerted their influence and expanded their power over a very large area for a very long time, primarily at the expense of the Christians. These two, the Christian challengers and the Muslim reformers have remained in conflict ever since. The balance of power between them has been swinging back and forth. The Jews continued to suffer until recently.[3]

Of course, none of these groups remained exclusively intact. Migration from one to the other has continued all the time. The Christian challengers themselves came originally from the Jewish originators. Their founder, Jesus Christ, was from among the Jews, and most of the early Christians were from the Jews. However, the later growth of Christians came from those who were alien to the Jews. These aliens, primarily the Europeans, ultimately became the dominant component of the Christian faith, and the faith was then redefined and reshaped into what essentially became a European faith – very different from the faith preached by Jesus Christ. Europeans would ultimately outnumber those who came from Abrahamic traditions by a large margin.

When the Muslims appeared on the scene, their numbers at first grew by the migration of the Jews and the Christians. Others from the east of the original location of the Muslims would also join their ranks and would ultimately outnumber those who came from the Abrahamic traditions by a large margin.

It is easily possible to concede the existence of the Ultimate Truth. But the Ultimate Truth can exist only and exclusively in the Divine Domain. Ultimate Truth belongs exclusively to God. No human can ever possess the

---

[3] So strong is the tendency for exclusivity that even Iqbal in his Reconstruction mentions Farid al-Din Attar not by his name but simply as "the great mystic poet of Islam", thus implying that Attar belongs exclusively to Islam.

Ultimate Truth or gain even a cursory understanding of it without Divine Will. Even the greatest of the prophets of God acquired access to only that part of the Ultimate Truth which God Himself decided to reveal to them.

This inquiry is an attempt to state that the Ultimate Truth, as much of it as is made accessible to humans, belongs to all on equal terms. Each human has equal opportunity to reach out and seek the Ultimate Truth and gain possession of as much of it as their effort and/or need justifies.

Ultimate Truth belongs to God. God belongs to all; to each and every human. There is no unique or absolute definition or description of God. Each human has the responsibility and the right to define and describe God in their own chosen way or style; whatsoever is the best way in which they can understand God. Each human also has the option to accept and adopt any available definition and description of God, or completely reject any and all definition and refuse to accept the idea of God. But nobody has the right to force a specific definition or description of God, or an idea against it, on anyone else. And nobody has the right to condemn anyone's chosen definition and description of God simply because it is different from their own definition. Organized human societies have an obligation to grant and to protect this right of choice for each human. The American Constitution guarantees it.

Individual choice is the manifestation of free will. All the colors that we have seen in this history come from the kaleidoscope of free will. Over the course of history, over multiple lands, and through myriads of times, the exercise of free will has generated mind-boggling results. The free will is like a seed; we do not know what fruits it will yield and what flowers will come out of it, till we know the hands that made themselves ready to sow it, the terrain in whose bosom it was laid to rest, the fountains that irrigated it, and the aroma of the air that cradled it.

Next chapter deals with the idea of Promised Land and Chosen People and explores from the Bible how these concepts are misunderstood and misused.

# 7. *Lessons from the Evolution of the Ideas of Chosen People and Promised Land*

*The identity of the Chosen People to whom the Land is promised in the Bible has kept on changing over time. The Promise was first to the seed of Abraham, then to the seed of Isaac, and then further narrowed down to the seed of Jacob, and so on. Those who now control what they call the Promised Land have gained control through their recently acquired power. A religious idea is thus shaped by the political and social exigencies of the time.*

The Forward of March 8, 2016, reported a Pew Research survey on the attitudes of Israeli Jews about the Arabs in Israel. That report is available at this link.[1]

The Forward reports: "Almost half of all Israeli Jews are in favor of transferring or expelling the state's Arab population, a major U.S. survey of Israeli public opinion has found. That staggering statistic comes from the Pew Research Center's report on Israel's religiously divided society, released on March 8."

Tamar Hermann, a professor at the Open University of Israel, reports Forward, said that the "word 'transfer' in this context means 'forceful expulsion, putting them on trucks and sending them away' across the Jordan River, to Jordan." The Forward further reported that the "topic has a long history in Israel, which is why it was included in the wide-ranging report. According to the research of historian Benny Morris, early Zionist leaders,

---

[1]     http://forward.com/news/israel/335292/48-of-israeli-jews-back-expulsion-or-transfer-of-arabs-new-pew-survey-says/#ixzz42L2nK5X5

73

including founding father David Ben Gurion, advocated for the transfer of Palestinians from the Jewish state."

This commonly held opinion, or desire, of a large segment of the Jewish Community generally manifests itself in, and is justified on the basis of, the concepts of the Promised Land and the Chosen People. The source for both of these claims is Torah in particular and Tanach in general. The Jewish claim to the exclusive ownership of the Land of Palestine – *Eretz Yisrael* – is based on Bible. But does the Bible Promise a Land to a certain people, and if so, who are these Chosen People? A careful reading of the Bible does not provide a definitive answer but does provide an opportunity for some analytical conclusions. Here is an attempt.

### The Promise – In summary

According to the Bible, the Book of Genesis, the Promise was first made to Abraham and repeated several times in his lifetime. But it was not delivered within his lifetime. When Sarah, his wife, died, he did not own any land in which to bury her. He had to buy a piece of land and Sarah was buried in it. Later Abraham was himself buried in the same land that he had bought.

The Promise was repeated to Isaac but was not delivered to him either. It was necessary to bury him in his father's burial place because he had no land of his own.

Then the Promise was repeated to Jacob but it was not delivered to him either. Jacob migrated to Egypt and died there. His remains were brought back and buried with his father and grandfather because he did not possess any land of his own, either in Egypt or in Canaan.

Moses was informed of the Promise and was told that it would be delivered through him. But it was not. Moses died without entering the Promised Land.

Joshua was told about the Promise and was commanded to proceed to take possession; God would be with him every step of the way. Joshua did occupy some land, but the Promise remained essentially unfulfilled.

Over two hundred years later, Saul and David were finally able to take possession of the Promised Land. It took 800 years for the Divine Promise to materialize.

Then it was lost within a little over 400 years.

A believer in God would acknowledge that God is supreme and all powerful, and nothing is beyond his power to accomplish. He is so powerful that when he wants something to happen, all He has to do is to command 'be' and it 'becomes'. "And God said, let there be light: and there was light".

It is not conceivable that God, with His infinite power, would keep on repeating the promise of land for 600 years from Abraham to Joshua, and be unable to deliver. Such outcome is not compatible with the Nature and Power of God.

Therefore, the repeated statements about the Promise cannot be Divine Pronouncements. This Promise, at best, is the human expression of the human wish in Divine Terms.

## The Chosen People

Through the pages of the Bible the definition of the Chosen People keeps on changing to become gradually narrower. It began with Abraham and the Chosen People were his seed. He had two sons and the older son Ishmael had to be eliminated. Therefore, the Chosen People became the seed of Isaac.

Isaac's first-born son Esau also had to be eliminated. That required the Chosen People to be further narrowed to the seed of Jacob.

When Jacob acquired the name Israel, the Chosen People became the Children of Israel. That remained the definition for a long time.

The purity of the holy seed was paramount. Anyone who violated that purity had to be eliminated. Kingdom of Israel was lost, and its people exiled and/or absorbed into other people, thus losing the 10 tribes. That reduced the community of the Chosen People to those living in the Kingdom of Judah. That population consisted of the tribes of Judah and Benjamin, part of Levi and the remnants of the other tribes who had settled in Judah. Over time, they were all absorbed into the dominant tribe of Judah, and when the name of the country was Latinized into Judea, they all became Judeans.

Later the term Judean was transformed into Jew.

Judah was conquered around 598-586 BCE and a large number of its citizens were taken as captives to Babylon. Iran conquered Babylon 50 years later, freed the captives and allowed them to return to Judah, if they so desired.

Not everyone wanted to return; 42,000 came back starting after 538 BCE and 80,000 stayed in Babylon. When they began to rebuild the Temple in Jerusalem, the people of the land, the abandoned poor, the *Am Ha'aretz*, who had been left behind when the elite were exiled to Babylon, wanted to participate.

They were Judeans or Jews who were not forced into exile. But the returnees rejected them and turned them away. Later when Ezra arrived, he defined the identity of the Chosen People in terms of the Babylonian Captivity and insisted on their strict separation from all other people, including the *Am Ha'aretz*. A proclamation was made "unto all the children of captivity, that they should gather themselves unto Jerusalem".[2] Ezra addressed the gathering. "You have transgressed, and have taken strange wives, to increase the trespass of Israel. Now therefore make confession unto the Lord, God of your fathers, and do his pleasure: and separate yourself from the people of the land and from the strange wives."[3]

People obeyed and a new definition of the community of the Chosen People was established. It was the holy seed among the children of captivity, purified by a strict separation from the people of the land – the *Am Ha'aretz* – and the removal of the abomination of intermarriage.

Those of the Children of Israel who did not suffer the trauma of exile were rejected and excluded. Later on, they became the Samaritans, or a major part of the Samaritan population.

Jews had been waiting for a Messiah. When Jesus, himself a Jew, came, the Jewish establishment rejected him, but the common Jewish people accepted him in large numbers. Initially Jesus was addressing primarily the Jews, and even said "I was sent only to the lost sheep of Israel."[4]

It may not be accurate to assume that Jesus wanted to restrict his message to the Jews only, but that is what his apostles initially did. If it was not for the bold initiative of Paul, the followers of Jesus may have remained a sect of Judaism. But Paul made it possible to spread the message far and wide and thereby established Christianity as a worldwide faith.

Paul was opposed by other apostles as is demonstrated by the "Incident at Antioch" where Peter, supported by Barnabas, refused to share a meal

---

[2] Ezra 10:7.
[3] Ezra 10:10-11.
[4] Matthew 15:24.

with the gentiles who had joined the followers of Jesus through Paul's preaching. Other apostles continued to preach to the Jews only and a large number of Jews in Palestine and elsewhere became Christians.

Under Roman rule after Constantine, most of the Children of Israel – the Chosen People – in Palestine were Christians.

When Arabs came to Jerusalem in 638, carrying their new faith with them, many Christians and Jews of Palestine turned to Islam and became Muslim. The Children of Israel, the purified Chosen People, the Holy Seed, thus became Christians and Muslims in large numbers.

No matter which definition of the Chosen People is used, the majority of them have long been Christians and Muslims who never left the territory called Canaan/Judah/Judea/Palestine/Israel. They have a stronger claim to the Promised Land than anyone else. Others may also belong to the community of the Chosen People, but they would have to prove their membership by following the standard set by Ezra. Then, they can share in the inheritance, but they cannot claim it exclusively.

***

# What does the Bible Say?
# The Detailed Information

'Abram the Hebrew'[5], also called Abraham, left Haran under God's Command to go to Canaan when he was 75 years old. In Canaan, the Lord told Abraham; "Unto your seed will I give this land".[6] A famine drove Abraham into Egypt but when he returned to Canaan, the Lord repeated his promise, "all the land that you see, I will give to you and to your seed forever".[7] Abraham wondered about the Lord's promise to his seed because he had no children, and said to the Lord, "what can you give me since I remain childless".[8] When the Lord told him that his seed would multiply in

---

[5] Genesis 14:13
[6] Genesis 12:7
[7] Genesis 13:15
[8] Genesis 15:2

numbers greater than the number of stars in the sky, as the dust of the earth, Abraham was still wondering and asked the Lord, "Lord God, whereby shall I know that I shall inherit it?".[9] The Lord repeated his promise again; "I have given this land to your seed, from the river of Egypt to the great river, the river Euphrates".[10]

This time the promise was made more definite with the phrase "I have given" and the area was more precisely defined.

The Lord God works in mysterious ways. After Abraham complained to the Lord about him being childless, his wife Sarah arranged for him to take a second wife Hagar, who is described in Chapter 16 of Genesis as "Egyptian", "handmaid", "Sarai's maid", and Sarah "gave her to her husband Abram to be his wife", saying "it may be that I may obtain children by her".[11] That concept of surrogate motherhood would be applied again later by both wives of Jacob, and is very similar to the old Hindu idea, found in Mahabharata, of a brother or sister fulfilling the obligation of a sibling for propagating the lineage. A believer, having read the background in the previous chapters, is likely to conclude that the Lord had something to do in motivating Sarah to take this action. Abraham was 85 years old at this time. A son was born to Abraham by Hagar when Abraham was 86 years old, and he named him Ishmael.

When Abraham was 99 years old, the Lord again repeated his promise of inheritance; "I will give to you and to your seed after you, the land in which you are a stranger, all the land of Canaan, for an everlasting possession; and I will be their God".[12] This time Canaan was named and the inheritance is promised for 'an everlasting possession'. At this time the only seed of Abraham was his one son Ishmael. Later that same year the Lord told Abraham about Sarah that "I will bless her and will give you a son by her", (Gen. 17:16). Abraham's immediate reaction was a deep concern for his first-born son; he said to the Lord, "If only Ishmael might live under your blessing!"[13]

---

[9] Genesis 15:8
[10] Genesis 15:18
[11] Genesis 16:2
[12] Genesis 17:8
[13] Genesis 17:18

The Lord answered Abraham's concern; "As for Ishmael, I have heard you; I have blessed him and will make him fruitful and multiply him greatly. He shall father twelve princes, and I will make him into a great nation".[14]

When Sarah displayed skepticism because of her advanced age, the Lord affirmed by declaring "Is anything too hard for the LORD?"[15] That is Biblical affirmation of God's infinite power. Sarah had a son when Abraham was 100 years old, and Sarah was 90. Abraham named that son Isaac and "made a great feast".[16] Sarah had herself given Hagar as wife to Abraham so she could have children through Hagar because she was not able to bear children herself. It was not Abraham's wish to marry Hagar. It was in fact Sarah who "gave her to her husband Abram to be his wife", because "it may be that I may obtain children by her".[17] By that statement and applying the principle of surrogate motherhood, Sarah had obtained a child by Hagar, who would, by that principle, be Sarah's child obtained by Sarah through Hagar. But now Sarah rejected not only Hagar but Sarah's own child whom she had obtained through Hagar as surrogate mother.

Here in Chapter 21, Hagar is now being called a bondwoman instead of wife which was the word used in Chapter 16. After Isaac was born, Sarah said unto Abraham, "Get rid of that slave woman and her son, for that woman's son will never share in the inheritance with my son Isaac".[18] The reaction of Abraham to Sarah's demand is very illuminating, as "this matter distressed Abraham greatly because it concerned his son Ishmael".[19] But after the Lord reassured Abraham that Ishmael would be protected and honored by the Lord, Abraham, who had ultimate obedience to the Lord, agreed to let Hagar and Ishmael to be sent away.

Once again, there is some confusion in the narrative. In 21:12 the Lord said that "it is through Isaac that your offspring will be reckoned". This appears to be an expression of Sarah's desire, and not that of the Lord, nor that of Abraham. Because in the very next verse 21:13, the Lord said that "I will make the son of the slave into a nation also, because he is your

---

[14] Genesis 17:20
[15] Genesis 18:14
[16] Genesis 21:8
[17] Genesis 16:2
[18] Genesis 21:10
[19] Genesis 21:11

offspring." If both are his sons, his offspring, his seed, then why is his progeny only through one of them?

Thus far the Lord had repeated His promise to Abraham at least four times that the land of Canaan would be given to him and his seed for an everlasting possession. But the actual possession of the Promised Land had not been delivered. When Sarah died at the age of 127, Abraham did not possess any land, not even a small piece of land in which to bury his wife. He was forced by necessity to buy the field and cave of Machpelah from Ephron the Hittite, the son of Zohar, for four hundred shekels of silver, for a burial ground.[20] Sarah was buried there. When Abraham died at the age of 175, he was also buried in the same place which he had bought.[21] Later Isaac and Jacob were also buried in the same place.[22]

The divine promise of the grant of land would be repeated to Isaac and he would also be told that his descendants would multiply to very large numbers. When another famine forced Isaac to want to go to Egypt, the Lord told him not to go. "Stay in this land for a while, and I will be with you and will bless you. For to you and your descendants I will give all these lands and will confirm the oath I swore to your father Abraham. I will make your descendants as numerous as the stars in the sky and will give them all these lands, and through your offspring all nations on earth will be blessed".[23] The promise had now been narrowed down to the seed of Isaac, and his older brother Ishmael was implicitly ignored and eliminated. But the promise would not be delivered in the lifetime of Isaac either.

Isaac had two sons, born as twins; Esau was the first born and Jacob was the second born. When Jacob was on his way to Haran to seek a wife, he stopped in some place one night and had a dream. In his dream he saw the Lord who said to him; "I am the LORD, the God of your father Abraham and the God of Isaac. I will give you and your descendants the land on which you are lying. Your descendants will be like the dust of the earth, and you will spread out to the west and to the east, to the north and to the south. All peoples on earth will be blessed through you and your offspring".[24] So, the land was now promised to Jacob, effectively removing his older

---

[20] Genesis 23:8-16
[21] Genesis 25:9
[22] Genesis 49:30-31 & 50:13
[23] Genesis 26:3-4
[24] Genesis 28:13-14

brother Esau from the promised inheritance. However, that promise would
not be delivered to Jacob either.

Jacob married the two daughters of his uncle Laban, Leah and Rachel.
Leah bore him four sons, but Rachel had no children. That situation would
repeat the story of Sarah and Hagar. Rachel said to Jacob; "Here is my
servant Bilhah; go into her, so that she may give birth on my behalf, that
even I may have children through her".[25] Bilhah bore two sons; that made
Rachel happy. Leah countered this in the same Sarah and Hagar tradition.
"When Leah saw that she had stopped having children, she took her servant
Zilpah and gave her to Jacob as a wife".[26] Two sons were born to Zilpah.
This time there was no jealousy, as Sarah had towards Hagar and her son.
Leah would later have two more sons and at least one daughter. Rachel
would also have two sons. That gave Jacob twelve sons in all from four
wives, and at least one daughter.

Only one daughter, Dinah, is named in the Bible but there is indication
that Jacob had other daughters, as implied by the phrase "all his daughters".[27]

All twelve sons were treated as equal by their family and the Hebrew
people of posterity. The four sons of Bilhah and Zilpah have always been
treated with the same honor as the six sons of Leah and the two sons of
Rachel. All have equal standing and together they have always been referred
to as the twelve tribes of Israel. They are known as the Children of Israel,
because Jacob had acquired Israel as another name.

Jacob prospered in Haran. Prosperity and wealth in those days were
measured both in material goods and in sons. Jacob was wealthy in both,
being father of 12 sons and owner of a large herd of cattle and other
material goods. But he possessed no land in spite of the repeated Divine
Promises over three generations. On his return from Haran, Jacob settled in
Shechem. "Jacob bought the plot of land where he camped from the family
of Hamor, the father of Shechem, for 100 pieces of silver. And there he
built an altar and named it El-Elohe-Israel."[28] But they were soon forced to
abandon Shechem because of a conflict with the people of Shechem and
had to move elsewhere. So, Jacob had lost even the small piece of land
which he had bought with money. Then, on their way, they stopped in

---

[25] Genesis 30:3-4
[26] Genesis 30:9
[27] Genesis 37:35
[28] Genesis 33:19-20

Bethel for a while. The Lord appeared to Jacob in Bethel and repeated the often-made promise; "The land that I gave to Abraham and Isaac I will give to you, and I will give the land to your seed after you".[29] This time the phrase "land that I gave to Abraham" is used even though it was never actually given to Abraham but only promised. There was still no indication of when this promise would be delivered.

Circumstances forced Jacob and his entire family to migrate to Egypt. They lived there until Moses got them out of Egypt. Moses, son of Amram, son of Kohath, son of Levi, son of Jacob. Moses is the fifth generation after Jacob.

Bible says, "All the persons of the house of Jacob who came into Egypt were seventy".[30] Since Bible only counts males, perhaps only adult males, the addition of all women and children, and all others who are usually referred to as servants and strangers, the total number of the house of Jacob might be around 300.

By the time of Moses, the Children of Israel, defined as the direct descendants of Jacob, had grown to a large number. They were the Chosen People as redefined and narrowed down at least twice. Moses conducted a census during the first year after Exodus, and another near the end of the 40-year journey through the Wilderness. Both times the men over 20 years of age, in all tribes except Levi, were counted. Each census yielded a number slightly over 600,000. By adding women and children, plus the house of Levi, and others to that number, the total population traveling through the Wilderness might have been a couple of million. Thus the 300 had multiplied to two million in five generations.

They crossed Jordan to begin to possess the land that the Lord had been promising them for over 600 years, without ever actually delivering it.

Moses died before crossing the river.

The Lord commanded Joshua "to cross the Jordan River into the land I am about to give to them – to the Israelites" and told Joshua; "I will give you every place where you set your foot, as I promised Moses".[31] Success was guaranteed by the Lord. "No one will be able to stand against you all

---

[29] Genesis 35:12
[30] Genesis 35:12
[31] Joshua 1:2-3

the days of your life. As I was with Moses, so I will be with you; I will never leave you nor forsake you".[32]

The Lord had already given instructions on how to proceed and what to do during the life of Moses. Joshua was required now to proceed under those rules and guidelines. The Lord had told the Israelites that "you shall dispossess the inhabitants of the land and dwell in it, for I have given you the land to possess".[33]

The Lord insisted on dispossessing the people who already lived in the land. "But if you do not drive out the inhabitants of the land, those you allow to remain will become barbs in your eyes and thorns in your sides. They will give you trouble in the land where you will live. And then I will do to you what I plan to do to them".[34]

The inhabitants of the land to be dispossessed were to be exterminated and no association with them was permitted. "When the LORD, your God, brings you into the land you are entering to possess and drives out before you many nations – the Hittites, Girgashites, Amorites, Canaanites, Perizzites, Hivites and Jebusites, seven nations larger and stronger than you – and when the LORD, your God, has delivered them over to you and you have defeated them, then you must destroy them totally. Make no treaty with them and show them no mercy. Do not intermarry with them. Do not give your daughters to their sons or take their daughters for your sons, for they will turn your children away from following me to serve other gods, and the LORD's anger will burn against you and will quickly destroy you".[35]

The reason was the superior status of the Children of Israel. "For you are a people holy to the LORD your God. The LORD your God has chosen you out of all the peoples on the face of the earth to be his people, his treasured possession".[36] The Lord had guaranteed victory and told the Israelites about what to do to the people "in the cities of the nations the LORD, your God, is giving you as an inheritance, do not leave alive anything that breathes. Completely destroy them – the Hittites, Amorites, Canaanites, Perizzites, Hivites and Jebusites - as the LORD, your God, has

---

[32] Joshua 1:5
[33] Numbers 33:53
[34] Numbers 33:55-56
[35] Deuteronomy 7:1-4
[36] Deuteronomy 7:6

commanded you".[37] Leave alive nothing that breathes; men, women, children, animals.

Under that mandate and under those guidelines, Joshua began his war of conquest and extermination. Jericho was attacked with a force of 40,000 men of war. The city was captured and they "completely destroyed everything in it with their swords – men and women, young and old, cattle, sheep, goats, and donkeys".[38] The city was so completely destroyed that it could not be built again. "Then they burned the whole city and everything in it, but they put the silver and gold and the articles of bronze and iron into the treasury of the LORD's house".[39]

Next was Ai. They made a miscalculation at first and suffered a setback. But it was quickly corrected, and Ai was attacked with a force of 30,000. "Then the LORD said to Joshua, 'Hold out toward Ai the javelin that is in your hand, for into your hand I will deliver the city."[40] Joshua obeyed the Lord and there was complete victory. "When Israel had finished killing all the men of Ai in the fields and in the wilderness where they had chased them, and when every one of them had been put to the sword, all the Israelites returned to Ai and killed those who were in it. Twelve thousand men and women fell that day – all the people of Ai. For Joshua did not draw back the hand that held out his javelin until he had destroyed all who lived in Ai."[41]

The Israelite Invasion Force of 30,000 men of war attacked Ai, whose total population, including men, women and children, was 12,000, and every one of them was killed.

The disparity in numbers was overwhelming. The Israelite fighting force consisted of over 600,000 people according to the two censuses. They were always able to attack with overwhelming numbers of fighting men; the size of the attack force frequently exceeded not only the size of the defending fighting force but often the whole population of the place under attack. The glowing accounts of victory after victory under the command of Joshua, while the Lord was with them every step of the way assuring their victory, would imply that they conquered the entire land of Canaan and possessed

[37] Deuteronomy 20:16-17
[38] Joshua 6:21
[39] Joshua 6:24
[40] Joshua 8:18
[41] Joshua 8:24-25

the Promised Land, flowing with milk and honey, in a very short time. Book of Joshua seems to give that impression. But the Book of Judges negates that impression and lowers the high expectations of the Book of Joshua.

The Children of Israel did come to the Promised Land, expecting to possess it, but possession was not delivered to them immediately. For that they would have to struggle for more than two hundred years; during which their fortunes fluctuated up and down.

All through this period, through good times and bad times, the Chosen People never made an effort nor expressed a desire, nor showed an inclination to make peace with the people of the land. They never made an attempt to co-exist with them. They remained steadfast in their desire to wipe these people out, repeatedly claiming that the Lord commanded it.

They believed that the Lord – their exclusive Lord, God of Israel – was doing the fighting Himself; and who can stand in front of the Lord! But, still, the goal was not achieved in the lifetime of Joshua or for over 200 years after him.

Saul became king around 1030 BCE. He began to unite the Israelites into one nation. That task was completed by David who united all of the tribes together, conquered Jerusalem, established a mighty empire, and finally caused the Promised Land to be delivered to the Chosen People, about 800 years after it was first promised. Solomon inherited that mighty empire, which commanded respect, prestige and admiration in the entire region. But Solomon's death marked the end of the empire built by Saul and David. A conflict immediately developed. The Empire split into two; Judah in the south contained two tribes; Israel in the north contained 10 tribes. Levi was in both.

The two kingdoms were at odds with each other throughout their existence, and their mutual conflict and friction cost them the prestige and respect that David had built. Israel existed for a little over two hundred years and was conquered and destroyed by Assyria in 722 BCE. All the prominent citizens of Israel were forcibly exiled into the northern territories of Assyria. They were absorbed into local populations over time. They are the Ten Lost Tribes of Israel. The poor laborers and peasants were left behind in Israel. Assyrians brought in people from the other territories in their Empire to settle in Israel to fill areas left vacant by those who had been forced into exile. The newcomers had the support of the Assyrian authorities. They enjoyed a privileged life and they subdued and overwhelmed the poor of Israel who were left behind and not forced into exile.

Judah existed a little longer but was finally conquered and destroyed by Babylon around 597 to 586 BCE. In two waves of forced exile, in 597 and 586, a large number of the elite of Judah, prominent citizens of nobility, wealth, knowledge and skill were forced to move to Babylon. Many of the other Judeans escaped the Babylonian oppressive rule by migrating to Egypt in a Reverse Exodus. Only the poor laborers and peasants were left behind, similar to what had happened in Israel over a hundred years before. People of the surrounding countries availed themselves of the opportunity to move into places vacated by those who were forcibly exiled to Babylon.

The Exiled People of Judah, however, did not meet the same fate as those exiled from Israel. In Babylon the Judeans found hardship but also opportunity. These Judeans were brought to Babylon because of their knowledge and skill. They used the opportunity to make something of themselves. When Cyrus of Iran conquered Babylon in 538 BCE, he freed the Jews and allowed them to return to Judah, if they so desired. Some took advantage of the opportunity and returned. But most did not.

In Babylon the exiles had worked very hard to preserve their identity. Having lost their land they turned to the one thing that distinguished them from their new neighbors, their sacred writings. They concentrated on developing and further enhancing their writings and refining their belief system. Important prophets helped them further define Judaism so that the Jews in Babylon had further refined their religion and made it much more advanced. The Babylonian Jews had also become prosperous in their new environment which they had adopted as their new home. Some of them had even adopted the Babylonian culture and the Babylonian way of life, including language and even names. And now, under Cyrus, they were free. When Cyrus allowed them to return, only 42,000 came back. The other 80,000 decided not to leave Babylon where a vibrant Jewish community remained for another 1,500 years. However, even those who stayed back helped the cause of the returnees with financial and material contributions.

Babylonian experience resulted in a very specific definition of Judaism and the Jew, which was bound to cause problems not only between the returning Jews and those who never had to leave Judah, but also, to some extent, within the returnees themselves. The returnees had to prove through genealogy that they belonged. Some "could not show that their families were descended from Israel".[42] Those belonging to the order of priesthood were also verified for legitimacy. Many "searched for their family records, but they could not find them and so were excluded from the priesthood as unclean".[43] That process decided who had the right to membership in the Jewish Community, and, among those so chosen, who could be priest. Many were disallowed to be part of the Jewish Community.

Next was the issue of the poor folk who had been abandoned and left in Judah during the Babylonian Exile; the *Am Ha'aretz*. They had maintained their faith as best as they could, but it was now very different from the advanced faith of the returnees. As the construction of the Temple was about to begin, the local people, the *Am Ha'aretz* – whom the Bible calls 'adversaries' – offered to join in the construction project. They were rejected and turned away.

This led to the question of who is and who is not entitled to membership in the Jewish Community. Those coming back from Babylon wanted to define the Jewish community entirely on the basis of the Babylonian Captivity. The chosen few were defined as the "children of captivity". 'Captivity' became a badge of Honor and the Defining Element of Faith, and a litmus test as to who can be called a Jew and can be included in the Jewish Community. This definition of a Jew based on 'Captivity' in Babylon, therefore, excluded everyone else who were not fortunate enough to be forced into captivity but were left behind in Judah to linger under the rule of the occupying forces.

It was observed and pointed out that the "people of Israel and the priests and the Levites have not separated themselves from the peoples of the lands with their abominations", and the "men of Israel have married women from these people and have taken them as wives for their sons. So, the holy race has become polluted by these mixed marriages. Worse yet, the leaders and officials have led the way in this outrage".[44]

Ezra came to the Temple to pray and "a large crowd of Israelites – men, women and children – gathered around him". One of them confessed to Ezra: "We have been unfaithful to our God by marrying foreign women from the peoples around us". It was suggested and all agreed to "make a

---

[42] Ezra 2:59
[43] Ezra 2:62
[44] Ezra 9:1-2

covenant before our God to send away all these women and their children".[45]
A new definition of the Jewish Community had emerged; it was based on
Babylonian captivity, separation from the people of the land, the *Am
Ha'aretz*, and the preservation of the holy seed, free from the 'abomination'
of intermarriage.

By the time of Jesus, Palestine had a large population of Jews as defined
by Ezra. The people of the land, the *Am Ha'aretz*, had by now come to be
known as the Samaritans. The whole area was occupied and ruled by the
Roman Empire, and there were a large number of Romans and Greeks,
both soldiers and civilians, all in positions of power and authority.

Jesus, himself a Jew, preached primarily to the Jews, even though he was
ready and willing to talk to anyone. All his Apostles were Jews and so were
almost all of his early followers. After Jesus, his apostles preached his
message, which they called "The Way", only to the Jews. They considered
themselves as Jews and were sincerely engaged in an effort to reform their
true faith in the light of the teachings of Jesus.

When Paul began to preach outside the Jewish community, to those
whom the Jews called the gentiles, other apostles were not happy about it.
This is best demonstrated by what is known as the "Incident at Antioch".
Through Paul's efforts many gentiles had accepted "The Way". But Peter,
who must have been in Antioch at the same time when Paul was also there
along with Barnabas, refused to share a meal with the gentile followers of
"The Way". Barnabas, who had been a companion of Paul up to that point,
sided with Peter. This led to a conflict between Peter and Paul.

If it was not for the continued efforts of Paul, "The Way" may never
have become Christianity, and may have remained a small sect of Judaism.

"The Way" did become Christianity and spread all over Middle East,
Europe and North Africa. Through the efforts of Peter and other apostles
in Judea, a large number of Judean Jews joined the new faith. While some
Jews were leaving Judea to escape Roman persecution, many of the Jews
who remained in Judea became Christians, though even they were also
persecuted at first.

After Constantine became a Christian, Jerusalem and Palestine became a
safe haven for the Christians to live, but the Jews were still persecuted. The

---

[45] Ezra 10:1-3

holy seed, purified by Ezra, was now flourishing in Jerusalem and Palestine as the Christian community.

By the time the Arabs came in 638 with their new faith, Christian descendants of Jacob were thriving in Palestine, and those Jews who were still in the area were oppressed. Arabs freed the Jews and allowed those Jews, who wanted to come back from areas they had been compelled to go, to return to Jerusalem and Palestine. Many came back to join those who were already there. Over the succeeding centuries many of the Children of Israel, most of whom were by then Christians, and some were Jews, turned to Islam. Except for the couple of centuries during the Crusades, Jerusalem and the surrounding regions remained under Muslim rule from 638 to 1918. Believers of the three faiths occupy Palestine and a large majority of them are descendants of Jacob but are either Christian or Muslim.

## Conclusion

A careful reading of the Bible does not lead to a definite conclusion that God had promised the land of Canaan to any particular group of humans. But if it is conceded that God did promise that land to a Chosen People, then the question arises as to their identity. The Biblical Community of the Chosen People, as has been seen, was originally defined as the Seed of Abraham, then successively narrowed down to the Seed of Isaac, then Seed of Jacob, known for many succeeding centuries as the Children of Israel. Finally, Ezra narrowed it down to the holy seed confined to the Children of Captivity defined by the Babylonian Captivity and purified of the 'abomination' of intermarriage. A substantial part of that community has remained in Palestine ever since the return from Babylon, and many of them became and have remained Christians after Jesus, and some became Muslims after 638. Those to whom the land was promised, if it was ever promised to anyone, are the Christians, Muslims and Jews who never left Palestine and have lived there over the last two millennia. Others can share in the inheritance but cannot claim it exclusively. According to the standard of Ezra, they need to establish through genealogy that they belong by showing "their father's house, and their seed, whether they were of Israel". (Ezra 2:59) And they must be purified of the 'abomination' of intermarriage.

The next chapter explores the concept of Messiah.

In Search of Meaning

# 8. Understanding Interfaith Commonalities - A Case Study of the Concept of Messiah

*The concept of a coming Messiah is common to the three Abrahamic faiths but has evolved along the culture-unique paths for Judaism, Christianity, and Islam. The psychological under- pinning and cultural dynamics continue to replay themselves in the recent history of the concept of Messiah.*

The concept of Messiah runs through the Abrahamic Religions. I analyze the concept in Judaism, Christianity, and Islam to explore a common theme dotted with differences of local historicity. I also examine this concept by looking into questions like how it originated in the context of the Jewish history, how it evolved as the history unfolded, and how the religious traditions and sociopolitical situations mutually intertwined. The objective is best served by a chronological view.

## Jewish Messiah

The tradition of Messiah among the Abrahamic religions started in the context of the Jewish history. When the Israelites were in bondage in Egypt, they wished for a Messiah who would deliver them from bondage and lead them to freedom. Moses arose among them and delivered them from bondage, leading them out of Egypt. The Hebrew people left Egypt around 1280[1] BCE, and, after spending 40 years in the wilderness of Sinai, crossed the river Jordan to enter Canaan around 1240 BCE. It was then that they began their quest to possess the land of Canaan, the Promised Land, the

---

[1]   Jewish   Virtual   Library,   Timeline   for   the   History   of   Judaism, www.jewishvirtuallibrary.org/jsource/History/timeline.html

land of milk and honey. According to Torah, that land had been promised[2] to Abraham and his children since the time of Abraham over 500 years before the Hebrews crossed Jordan into Canaan. The Lord had promised[3] that He would Himself deliver this land into the exclusive possession of the Hebrew people. With the Lord, God of Israel, guiding them every step of the way, it would take the Hebrew people over 200 years to finally control most of the Promised Land, and to establish, around 1000 BCE, the Kingdom of Judah with Jerusalem as its capitol[4]. Within a century, the Kingdom would split into two, when, around 931 BCE, the North separated from Judah to establish the Kingdom of Israel with Samarra as its capitol[5]. The Hebrew domination of the Promised Land lasted for about 300 years. Then things began to turn bad for them. First, the Assyrians destroyed the Kingdom of Israel in the North[6] around 722 BCE. Then the Babylonians destroyed the Kingdom of Judah in the South around 587 BCE and destroyed the First Temple.

### The Need for Messiah

In bad times people begin to wish for help from the unknown regions and begin to hope for the appearance of a Savior, a Messiah, a Deliverer. After the Babylonians conquered and enslaved the Jews and destroyed their Temple, the Jewish people were facing bad times. They began to wish for a Savior, a Messiah, who would lead them back to days of glory. The later Biblical writings contain references to this wish in the form of predictions of the coming of a Messiah[7]. These predictions spelled out the conditions which would induce the Messiah to come, who he would be in terms of his family lineage, and what he would accomplish when he finally arrived[8].

---

[2] Genesis 15:18-21 "On that day the Lord made a covenant with Abram and said, "To your descendants I give this land, from the Wadi of Egypt to the great river, the Euphrates — the land of the Kenites, Kenizzites, Kadmonites, Hittites, Perizzites, Rephaites, Amorites, Canaanites, Girgashites and Jebusites."

[3] Joshua 1:1-6

[4] 2 Samuel 5:1-12

[5] 1 Kings 12:1-20

[6] Marc Zvi Brettler, "The Creation of History in Ancient Israel", ISBN 9780415194075, Routledge, 1998.

[7] Babylonian Talmud: Tractate Sanhedrin Folio 98a

[8] He would be a descendant of Jacob through Judah, (Numbers 24:17); would be born to a Virgin (Isaiah 7:14); would be born in the city of Bethlehem (Micah 5:2).

One of their own did rise, and his birth and life did initiate a new age. Jesus declared that he had come to remind his people, the twelve tribes of Israel, to return to the law as given to them by the Lord through Moses and later Prophets, because, as he said, his people had forgotten the law or had corrupted it[9]. Some of his people accepted him and became his followers. But the establishment along with many others of his people rejected him and turned against him. After he was gone, the number of his followers continued to rise, but mostly outside the Hebrew community. His followers called him Jesus Christ, the Messiah and the Savior, and called themselves the Christians. They elevated Jesus to be Divine, called him the only begotten Son of God, and therefore God[10]. Christian Faith would spread far beyond the land of Palestine in which Jesus preached his message and would become the religion of almost all of Europe, and through European expansion, of the new world in North and South Americas, Sub-Saharan Africa, and Asia Pacific[11].

**The Search Continued**

Jews were waiting for Messiah. When Jesus came, many accepted him, but many others rejected him. Those who rejected him kept on waiting for Messiah. Another possibility would arise within a little over a century.

The land of Jews had been occupied by a succession of invaders; the Assyrians, the Babylonians, the Greeks, and the Romans. Jews never fully accepted to live under occupation and continued to struggle to regain their independence. They rose against Rome in the year 66 of the Common Era[12] – the era initiated by the arrival of the Messiah whom the Jews had mostly rejected. The struggle failed. They were crushed by the Romans, who destroyed the Temple and made it difficult for Jews to live in and around Jerusalem.

The Jews would rise again around 132. This time they were led by a very capable general, Shimon Ben Kosibah, under whose leadership the struggle

---

[9] Matthew 23:23-39.

[10] John 3:16 "For God so loved the world that he gave his only Son, that whoever believes in him should not perish but have eternal life."

[11] Pew Research Center, Religion and Public Life, Regional Distribution of Christians http://www.pewforum.org/2011/12/19/global-christianity-regions/

[12] Hershel Shanks (ed.), "Ancient Israel: From Abraham to the Roman Destruction of the Temple", ISBN-13: 978-0205096435, Prentice Hall, Biblical Archeology Society, 3rd edition, 2010.

achieved a measure of success for some time[13]. Rabbi Akiva gave him the name "Bar Kokhba" meaning "Son of a Star" from the Star Prophecy verse[14]. People called him Bar Kokhba, and many accepted him as messiah. He took the title of Nasi Israel and ruled over the country that was virtually independent for two and a half years; it minted its own coins. But the glory was short lived. Romans crushed the revolt, killed a large number of Jews, destroyed hundreds of Jewish villages, expelled Jews from Jerusalem, and changed the name of the land to Palestine to dissociate it from Jewish identity. Shimon Ben Kosibah was killed in the fighting. After the failure of the revolt, people turned against the man they thought was a Messiah. Some even referred to him as "Simon bar Kozeba" meaning "Son of lies" or "Son of deception". As the saying goes, people worship the rising sun; after it goes down, most everyone turns against it. They were with him when he was winning. But turned against him when he lost the war and his life.

Jews continued to wait for the Messiah. Over time, the concept of Messiah went through a good degree of intellectual transformation giving rise to Messianic Jews[15]. The idea of a Messiah slowly became the hope for a Messianic Age[16], when all faithful together will bring about an atmosphere in which humans will live a happy and prosperous life. As such, each person would contain and possess elements of the personality of a Messiah.

Even the Christians and the Muslims are waiting for a Messiah, who may or may not be the same, and may not be the one that Jews are waiting for. The differences and similarities are attributable to the societal situations of each group, as is discussed below.

## Christian Messiah

Christians believe that Jesus died on the Cross, was resurrected to life and in his second life ascended to heavens where he has been ever since[17].

---

[13] John S. Evans (2008). "The Prophecies of Daniel 2", Known as the Bar Kokhba Revolt, after its charismatic leader, Simon Bar Kokhba, whom many Jews regarded as their promised messiah.

[14] Numbers 24:17: "There shall come a star out of Jacob."

[15] Messianic Jews https://en.wikipedia.org/wiki/Messianic_Judaism

[16] Isaiah 9:1-7

[17] Hebrews 9:27-30 "Just as people are destined to die once, and after that to face judgment, so Christ was sacrificed once to take away the sins of many; and he will appear a second time, not to bear sin, but to bring salvation to those who are waiting for him."

Hebrews 10:12-13 "But when this priest had offered for all time one sacrifice for

According to the Book of Revelation in the Christian Bible, Jesus will return to earth to establish the Kingdom of God[18]. The conditions that will induce him to come, the manner in which he will come, and what he will do when he finally comes are perceived to be well defined[19]. Every now and then, there is a discussion about the prevailing human conditions that are considered to be appropriate for the second coming of Jesus. However, the benefit of the return of Jesus and the Kingdom that he would establish is only for those with faith in Jesus Christ as the Savior[20].

In the view of most Christians, Jesus has not yet returned, though many others have appeared and have made major contributions to the development and transformation of Christian Faith. More than one such persons appeared in Europe during the sixteenth century: Martin Luther in Germany, John Calvin in France, and John Knox in Scotland. In the 19th century, Joseph Smith appeared in the USA. He declared himself to be a Prophet and founded the Church of Latter-Day Saints. These reformers changed the Christian religion in an essential way.

Until that time, almost all Christians belonged to one of the two Churches; the Catholic Church based in Rome, and the Orthodox Church based in Constantinople, now called Istanbul. Almost all of Europe was Christian, and Western Europe belonged to the Catholic Church.

Religion played a very important part in the life of people at all levels of society, including the Royal Families and the Kings; and the conduct of the rulers was closely governed by the rules of the church. Pope enjoyed political supremacy over the entire Western Roman Empire and continued to play a powerful role in Western Europe, often competing with monarchs for control over wide-ranging affairs of Church and state, crowning emperors, and regulating disputes among secular rulers. Even after its political influence had diminished, the Catholic Church and the Pope

---

sins, he sat down at the right hand of God, and since that time he waits for his enemies to be made his footstool."

[18] Mathew 24:30 "Then the sign of the Son of Man will appear in heaven, and then all the tribes of the earth will mourn, and they will see the Son of Man coming on the clouds of heaven with power and great glory."

[19] Mathew 24

[20] Acts 4:11-12. "Jesus is the stone you builders rejected, which has become the cornerstone. Salvation is found in no one else, for there is no other name under heaven given to mankind by which we must be saved."

continued to be the supreme authority over all religious and spiritual matters with some notable exceptions due to the contributions of the above-mentioned reformers.

**Messiah amongst Muslims**

The concept of Messiah does not conflict with Muslim ideology. However, Muslim doctrine of the Finality of God's Message, as delivered through Muhammad, implied that God would no longer directly speak to, or make a direct contact with, any human until the Day of Judgment. In this context, a prophet is elevated above a messiah. That condition of Muslim doctrine held worldwide for longer than a thousand years. No person of significant stature made a claim to have spoken to God or to have received a direct revelation or inspiration from God.

It changed in the nineteenth century when four persons in succession would each claim that God had spoken to them. The first of them was Joseph Smith; the other three are discussed below.

**Background**

The Shia Muslim doctrine holds that a living Imam, who must be a direct descendent of the Prophet, has exclusive domain over the religious, spiritual and political leadership of the Muslim Community[21]. Muhammad had sons but they died as infants. He had four daughters; two of them had no children, one had a child who died young, and the fourth daughter, Fatima, who was married to Ali, had two sons and one daughter. The only descendants of Muhammad are from his youngest daughter Fatima and son-in-law Ali.

Fatima holds a position of high honor in the Shia community, and Ali is regarded as the rightful inheritor of leadership of the Muslim community after Muhammad. This is so because in a patriarchal society one cannot even think of a daughter – even if she is the only child – succeeding her father. The Sunni Muslims do not subscribe to this requirement for the leadership of Muslim Community, and that is the primary difference between the two. However, Sunni Muslims also hold Fatima and Ali with high regard, except they do not recognize their claim to the exclusive

---

[21] Seyyed Vali Reza Nasr, "The Shia revival: how conflicts within Islam will shape the future (1st ed.)", ISBN 0-393-06211-2, New York: Norton, 2006.

leadership of the Muslim Community simply by virtue of their blood relation to the Prophet.

Ali is the first Shia Imam. Succession, in Shia belief, had to be through his direct descendants. These Imams, after Ali, never were able to achieve political power and leadership, but they and their followers opposed the prevailing rulers and declared them to be the illegitimate usurpers of power because they did not descend from the Prophet[22]. The Imams and their followers were considered by the rulers, who were Sunni, as dangerous troublemakers. There was a constant struggle between the Imams and the power structure. Many Imams died mysteriously, some even in prison.

The twelfth Imam, Muhammad ibn al-Hassan al-Mahdi, became Imam around the age of four when his father, the previous Imam, died. Soon thereafter, Imam Muhammad disappeared mysteriously. His followers proclaimed that he had gone into hiding because the time and circumstances were not suitable for his work. But he would return under more suitable conditions[23].

Imam Muhammad ibn al-Hassan al-Mahdi disappeared around 872, is supposed to have never died and is believed by his followers to be still living. A great deal has been written about him, about why and how he disappeared, under what circumstances he would return, how he would be recognized when he finally appeared, and what he would do and how he would do it.

It is primarily a Shia belief, but the story has been developing for over a thousand years and has continued to grow in power and mystery. The coming of Mahdi has been proclaimed to have been foretold by the Prophet himself[24]. Therefore, most Muslims, both Shia and Sunni, are waiting for the Mahdi. Christians had been waiting for the return of Jesus even longer. Those waiting for Mahdi have combined the appearance of Mahdi with the return of Jesus. This combined event has over time been accepted, in varying degrees, throughout the Muslim Community, Shia and Sunni both.

Most of the Muslims are now waiting for the appearance of Mahdi who will fight and defeat the Anti-Christ, known as Dajjal by Muslims, and pave the way for the return of Jesus. Mahdi will welcome and greet Jesus on his

---

[22] Saunders, "A History of Medieval Islam", Rutledge and Kegan Paul Ltd, 1965

[23] Abdulaziz Abdul Hussein Sachedina. "Islamic Messianism: The Idea of Mahdi in Twelver Shiism". ISBN 9780873954426, Suny press. 1981.

[24] See for example Sunan Ibn Majah, Vol. 2, Tradition #4086.

return and will work with him to establish the Kingdom of God. But, in the Muslim view, this kingdom of God, to be established by Jesus with the help of Mahdi, would be for the exclusive benefit of Muslims.

## Bab

The largest segment of the Shia Muslims is known as the Twelvers because they believe in Twelve Imams. The Twelvers believe that even after the twelfth Imam went into occultation around 872, he continued to communicate through a mediator, called Bab (Arabic for gate or door). He had appointed more than one Babs in succession, till he ceased to communicate around 940[25]. The Twelvers believe that the Hidden Imam is alive in the world, but in concealment from his enemies, and would emerge just before the Day of Judgment. He will emerge as the Qaim (he who will rise) and acting as the Mahdi (he who is rightly guided) will start a holy war against evil, defeat the unbelievers and establish a reign of justice.

Many have claimed to be Mahdi but the first person who developed a substantial following was Siyyid Ali Muhammad (1819-1850), a Shia Muslim. He was a merchant from Shiraz, Iran. In 1844, he claimed that he was the Bab. That would mean that the Hidden Imam Muhammad ibn al-Hassan, who had ceased communications around 940, had resumed to communicate after about 900 years, and had appointed Siyyid Ali Muhammad as the current Bab. Later, he began explicitly to proclaim that he was not merely the Bab to the Hidden Imam, but the Manifestation of the Hidden Imam himself. He claimed to be the Qaim, the Mahdi, and the new messenger from God with divine authority because God spoke to him.

In a sequence very similar to how John the Baptist announced the arrival of Jesus Christ, the Bab, in most of his prominent writings, alluded to the Promised One, most commonly referred in Arabic as *man-yazhiruhu'lláh*, "he whom God shall make manifest". He claimed that he himself was "but a ring upon the hand of the one Whom God shall make manifest".

Bab was a Shia Muslim and was claiming to fulfill a Shia Prophecy. He did gain some following. However, he and his followers were rejected and strongly opposed both by the Shia religious establishment and by the Shia Iranian government. He was accused of heresy and tried in a court of law. Authorities admonished him to recant his claims, but there is no clear

---

[25] Andrew J. Newman, "Twelver Shiism: Unity and Diversity in the Life of Islam, 632 to 1722", ISBN 978-0-7486-7833-4, Edinburgh University Press. 2013.

evidence that he did. He was convicted, sentenced to death, and executed in 1850. This would later give rise to the Baha'i movement.

## Bahaullah

Within a few years of the Báb's death, over 25 persons would claim to be the Promised One. But Mirza Husain Ali Nuri (1817-1892) was accepted most widely as the Promised One, and ultimately came to be recognized as the prophetic fulfillment of Babism. He was a Shia Muslim from Tehran, Iran. Born in 1817, he was two years older than the Bab. He accepted the Báb's claim, became a Babi and helped to spread Babism, especially in his native province of Nur. He was recognized as one of the most influential believers of Babism. The Babis were being persecuted by authorities in Iran and many were imprisoned in various places. Mirza Husain Ali was also imprisoned in 1852. He was released from prison in 1853 but was exiled from Iran. He chose to go to Baghdad, Iraq[26]. At that time, an increasing number of Babis considered Baghdad the new center for leadership of Babism.

Mirza Husain Ali adopted the title Bahaullah, Arabic for 'Glory of God', and that is the name by which he is now known. According to Bahaullah, in 1852, while a prisoner in Tehran, he had several mystical experiences and visions, which symbolically marked the beginning of his mission as the next Báb. Ten years later, in 1863 in Baghdad, he made a formal proclamation to a small group of his companions, declaring that God spoke to him. Then in 1866, Bahaullah publicly made his claim to be "He Whom God Shall Make Manifest". Eventually he was recognized by the vast majority of Babis as the Promised One, and "He whom God shall make manifest". His followers began calling themselves Bahais.

Bahaullah subsequently declared that he was the "Promised One" of all religions, fulfilling the messianic prophecies found in all world religions. Bahaullah's eschatological claims constitute six distinctive messianic identifications:

from Judaism, the incarnation of the "Everlasting Father" from the Yuletide prophecy of Isaiah 9:6, and the "Lord of Hosts" of Isiah 47:4.

---

[26] Encyclopedia Iranica, http://www.iranicaonline.org/articles/bahaism-i

from Christianity, the "Spirit of Truth" or Comforter predicted by Jesus
in his farewell discourse of John 14:17 and the return of Christ "in
the glory of the Father".

from Zoroastrianism, the return of Shah Bahram Varjavand, a
Zoroastrian messiah predicted in various late Pahlavi texts.

from Shi'a Islam the return of the Third Imam, Imam Husain.

from Sunni Islam, the return of Jesus (Isa); and

from Babism, "He whom God shall make manifest".

Within Iran there was a strong rejection of Bahaullah and the Bahais, just
as there had been a rejection of the Báb and the Babis. But the movement
and their leader were in Baghdad, Iraq, and therefore beyond the reach of
the Shia Iranian authorities. The Sunni authorities of the Ottoman Empire
did not react as violently to the claim of being the Bab, or the Mahdi, but
the claim of being a messenger of God did not sit well with them. In time,
the Bahais would be forced to make a choice; continue to call themselves
Muslim and face persecution or call themselves something else. Ultimately,
they gave up any connection to Islam and began to refer to their faith as a
new faith started by Bahaullah. By now, Bahais do not even remember, and
do not care to be reminded, that their faith began within Islam.

## Ghulam Ahmad

A couple of decades after Bahaullah declared himself to be the Promised
One, and within his lifetime, rose a Messiah in Punjab, India. Mirza Ghulam
Ahmad declared in 1889 that he was the Promised Messiah, the second
coming of Jesus, the Reformer of the Age, the Mahdi awaited by Muslims,
and a Prophet of God[27]. He declared that God spoke to him and that he
was making his claim on Divine authority. Since the finality of Prophet-
hood in Muhammad was of paramount importance to Muslims, he did not
challenge that finality but modified it. He created a differentiation between a
law-bearing prophet and a non-law-bearing prophet and declared that Islam
had been completed and perfected in Muhammad and the complete and
perfect Law of God was contained in the Qur'an. No law-bearing prophet
would come after Muhammad and Qur'an cannot be altered or modified.
However, non-law-bearing prophets can come after Muhammad in order to

[27] Adil Hussain Khan, "From Sufism to Ahmadiyya: A Muslim Minority Movement in
South Asia", ISBN 978-0-253-01523-5, Indiana University Press, Bloomington, 2015.

reform and strengthen Islam. These prophets would be subordinate to Muhammad, the last law-bearing prophet.

Thus, Mirza Ghulam Ahmad, according to his claim and the belief of his followers, is a non-law-bearing prophet who is subordinate and deputy to Muhammad, and whose advent is the continuation of the prophet-hood of Muhammad.

The distinction of law-bearing and non-law-bearing prophets did not, however, find any acceptance among the mainstream Muslim community. Their strongest objection was to his claim that God speaks to him. To complicate matters further, his son, Mirza Basheer-ud-Din Mahmood Ahmad, after his father's death, declared that any Muslim who does not accept his father as a prophet is a rejecter of faith and therefore not a Muslim. The mainstream Muslim community has strongly rejected such claims and considers his followers to be heretic[28].

The movement attracted some followers in Punjab and other parts of India. It also carried its mission overseas and found greater success there than it found in India.

Unlike the Bahais, who under persecution decided to give up their claim to Islam and severed their connection to Islam, Ahmadis have refused to give up their claim to Islam. They continue to insist that they are Muslim and claim to practice Islam in its pristine form. They hold that Islam is the final law for humanity as revealed to Muhammad and they have been assigned the task of restoring it to its true essence and pristine form, which had been lost through the centuries.

## Conclusion

The concept of Messiah has its roots in the Jewish tradition. During the days of bondage in Egypt, the Hebrews wished and waited for a Messiah who would deliver them from bondage. Moses delivered them from bondage and set them on their path to days of glory in Canaan, the Promised Land, the land of milk and honey. The days of glory do not last forever for anyone. They ended for the Hebrews in their enslavement by the Assyrians and the Babylonians. Once again, they began to wish for a Messiah, a Deliverer. In time, other Abrahamic religions would join the Hebrews in wishing for a Messiah, namely the Christians and Muslims. Every segment would have their own definition of who the Messiah would

---

[28] Abul Ala Maududi, "The Qadiani Problem", Islamic Publications, Lahore, 1953.

be, what he would do, and for whose benefit. Many Messiahs appeared over time; each was accepted by some and rejected by others. The dynamics of these evolutions were driven by the particular geopolitics of the land and the communities.

Next chapter zooms in on a single case study, that of the Islamic scripture, to explore how a single researcher views it versus a government appointed committee. It illustrates how different settings influence the exercise of free will.


**Acknowledgement:** My brother, Dr. Abdur Rahim Choudhary, collaborated in the research and the writing of this chapter, with a very meaningful contribution.

# 9. Lost in Translation: the Curious Case of Saudi Revision of Abdullah Yusuf Ali's Translation of the Quran

*Abdullah Yusuf Ali's English translation of Quran was meant to have a universal appeal, a progressive direction, and to be free from apparent contradictions between the scientific and the religious world views. In 1980 the Saudi Arabian authorities decided to use his translation for worldwide distribution, and in the process revised it to conform it to their traditional and regressive interpretation of the Holy Book. The case shows how political powers and the religious establishment shape religious narrative and exercise social control.*

The Tafsir of the Qur'an in English by Abdullah Yusuf Ali (1872-1953), a renowned Muslim scholar from India, was published in 1934 under the title The Holy Qur'an: Text, Translation and Commentary. It became widely accepted around the world wherever English was spoken and read. When the Saudis decided around 1980 to create a 'better' English translation of the Qur'an, they actually ended up using primarily the work of Abdullah Yusuf Ali, to which they made some modifications. This is an attempt to review how that effort came about. In this analytical look at the Saudi modification of the translation and commentary by Abdullah Yusuf Ali, an attempt is made to understand the goals of Abdullah Yusuf Ali in making his gigantic effort to which he dedicated 40 years of his life. The stated goals of the Saudi effort are also studied with a view to assess how successful was that effort in accomplishing those goals. This analysis also aims to study the impact of the Saudi effort on what Abdullah Yusuf Ali was trying to accomplish.

The Saudi Authorities, desirous of a perfect English translation of the Qur'an, selected the translation and commentary of Abdullah Yusuf Ali and revised it, purportedly to 'correct' what they considered to be errors. The revised edition was first published under the Saudi Authority without credit to the original translator. It is now being published all over the world under the name of Abdullah Yusuf Ali. While the current editions have restored some or all of the introductory and explanatory notes of Abdullah Yusuf Ali, which the Saudi edition had removed, the contents are not the original work of Abdullah Yusuf Ali, but they are the Saudi revised version. In addition, Abdullah Yusuf Ali had included fourteen (14) Appendices to discuss and elaborate various subjects. Saudi Editors deleted three (3) of them; 6, 8 and 12. All current editions are also missing those three Appendices.

Appendix VI:      Allegorical Interpretation of the Story of Joseph
Appendix VIII:   Mystic Interpretation of the Verse of Light
Appendix XII:    The Muslim Heaven

Saudi revised version, with these and other significant changes, is now being published by Amana Publications, all over the world under the name of Abdullah Yusuf Ali, as if it is the original work.

## Translations of the Qur'an

Qur'an has been translated into just about every language of the world, but many among the Muslims are not at ease with the idea of translating it into any language other than the original Arabic. During the first couple of hundred years of Islam, there were no translations of Qur'an into any other language except the translation of the first chapter into Farsi made by Salman Farsi. Perhaps there was no need, because Arabic was spoken in all places.

Some translations were finally made into Sindhi and Hindi during the later part of the ninth century as Muslim population began to grow in some parts of India. A Greek translation is believed to have been made in the ninth century. It is not available now, but it is known to have been used by Nicetas Byzantius, a scholar from Constantinople, in his 'Refutatio' written between 855 and 870.

Muslims generally hold that only the original Arabic is the Qur'an. The Catholic Church had taken the same attitude when it did not permit any translation of the Bible from Greek or Latin into any local languages such as German or English, on the pain of death. Most Muslims would be strongly opposed to referring to any translation as the Qur'an. Many insist on using some other descriptive term such as 'the meaning of the Qur'an' or something like that. That is what Pickthal, an Englishman, called his translation, 'The Meanings of the Glorious Qur'an'.

The expanding Muslim population way beyond the Arabic speaking people has made it essentially necessary to translate it, so as to make it accessible to those who do not know Arabic. By now, Muslims outside the Arabic speaking population account for 85% of all Muslims. And they need to know the teachings of their Holy Book. Therefore, translations are made into all languages because Muslims are living all over the world and are speaking just about every language.

In his Note on 'Translation of the Qur'an'[1], Abdullah Yusuf Ali has noted the Urdu translations by Shah 'Abdul Qadir of Delhi (d 1826), Shah Rafi'-ud-din of Delhi, Shah Ashraf 'Ali Thanwi, and Maulvi Nazir Ahmad (d. 1912). He did not think that they were very good.

He has provided in much detail the European attempts to translate the Qur'an in various European languages. A Latin translation was made about 1143 but not published at that time because it was for the internal personal use of Peter the Venerable, Abbot of Clugny. It was entitled *Lex Mahumet pseudoprophete* ("The law of Mahomet the false prophet"). It was finally published in 1543 with a preface by Martin Luther and was later translated into Italian, German, and Dutch. Salomon Schweigger made a German translation which was published at Nuremburg in 1616. A French translation by Andre Du Ryer was published at Paris in 1647. It was re-translated into other languages, most notably into English by Alexander Ross in 1649. Savary's French translation appeared in 1783, and Kasimirski's French translation first appeared in 1840. The Germans followed up Schweigger with Boysen's translation in 1773, Wahl's in 1828, and Ullmann's in 1840.

---

[1] **Abdullah Yusuf Ali**. The Holy Qur'an; Text, Translation and Commentary: Abdullah Yusuf Ali – Printed in the United States by McGregor & Werner, Inc. 1946: Translation of the Qur'an, page xv.

Ludovico (or Luigi or Lewis) Maracci (1612-1700) was Confessor to Pope Innocent XI and a teacher of Arabic. He translated Qur'an; it was published in 1698 with Arabic text along with translation into Latin and his annotations. He added an essay titled "Refutation of the Qur'an", in which Marracci attempted to disprove Islam from the Catholic point of view. Abdullah Yusuf Ali noted that Marraci's work contained "quotations from various Arabic Commentaries, carefully selected and garbled, so as to give the worst possible impression of Islam to Europe. Maracci was a learned man, and there is no pretense about the object he had in view, viz., to discredit Islam by an elaborate show of quotations from Muslim authorities themselves. Maracci was himself a Confessor to Pope Innocent XI; his work is dedicated to the holy Roman Emperor Leopold I; and he introduces it by an introductory volume containing what he calls a "Refutation of the Qur'an."[2] Marracci's translation also became a source of many other European renderings of the Qur'an, including the French rendering by Savary and one in German by Nerreter. It was also the source of the English version prepared by George Sale in 1734.

Abdullah Yusuf Ali had this to say about the European renderings of the Qur'an. "The first English translation by A. Ross was but a translation of the first French translation of Du Ryer of 1647 and was published a few years after Du Ryer's. George Sale's translation (1734) was based on Maracci's Latin version, and even his notes and his Preliminary Discourse are based mainly on Maracci. Considering that Maracci's object was to discredit Islam in the eyes of Europe, it is remarkable that Sale's translation should be looked upon as a standard translation in the English-speaking world, and should pass through edition after edition, being even included in the series called the Chandos Classics and receiving the benediction of Sir E. Denison Ross. The Rev. J. M. Rodwell arranged the Suras in a rough chronological order. His translation was first published in 1861. Though he tries to render the idiom fairly, his notes show the mind of a Christian clergyman, who was more concerned to "show up" the Book than to appreciate or expound its beauties. Prof. E. H. Palmer's translation (first published in 1876) suffers from the idea that the Qur'an ought to be

---

[2] **Abdullah Yusuf Ali**. The Holy Qur'an; Text, Translation and Commentary: Abdullah Yusuf Ali – Printed in the United States by McGregor & Werner, Inc. 1946: Translation of the Qur'an, page xv.

translated into colloquial language. He failed to realize the beauty and grandeur of style in the original Arabic. To him that style was "rude and rugged": we may more justifiably call his translation careless and slipshod."[3]

## The Method and the Purpose of the European Translations

European attempts at the translation of the Qur'an were made with the specific purpose to discredit it by trying to show it to be 'false'. Even so, most of the people were fiercely opposed to these translations. There was legal action to block the publication, in 1649, of the translation attributed to Alexander Ross, who may or may not have actually done the translation. But he did write an essay titled 'Needful Caveat' and attached it to the publication. In that 'Caveat' he addressed the Christian Reader to say: "THERE being so many Sects and Heresies banded together against the Truth, finding that of Mahomet wanting to the Muster, I thought good to bring it to their Colors, that so viewing thine enemies in their full body, thou may the better prepared to encounter, and I hope, to overcome them. It may happily startle thee, to find him so to speak English, as if he had made some Conquest on the Nation; but thou wilt soon reject that fear, if thou consider that this his Alcoran, (the Ground-work of the Turkish Religion) hath been already translated into almost all Languages in Christendom, (at least, the most general, as the Latin, Italian, French, &c.) yet never gained any Proselyte, where the Sword, its most forcible and strongest argument, hath not prevailed".

His goal was to pacify the opposition to the publication by making it clear that the publication would help the Christians to understand their enemies, 'the Muslims' and be better prepared to overcome the 'enemy'. In the next paragraph he adds; "Thou shalt find it of so rude, and incongruous a composure, so farce with contradictions, blasphemies, obscene speeches, and ridiculous fables, that some modest, and more rational Mahomedans have thus excused it; that their Prophet wrote an hundred and twenty thousand sayings, whereof three thousand only are good, the residue (as the impossibility of the Moons falling into his sleeve, the Conversion and Salvation of the Devils, and the like) are false and ridiculous."[4]

---

[3] Ibid, page xv.
[4] **The Alcoran of Mahomet**: Translated out of Arabique into French by the Sieur Du Ryer, Lord of Malezair, and Resident for the King of France at Alexandria, and Newly Englished for the Satisfaction of All That Desire to Look into Turkish Vanities, to Which

Until the time of this publication, Europe knew Islam only through their acquaintance with the Ottoman Empire, with whom they were often at war. They knew Islam to be the religion of the Turks and learned about it from them.

The critical comments by Abdullah Yusuf Ali about the English rendering of the Qur'an by George Sale (1697-1736) are fully justified. His translation, published in 1734, is held in such high regard in Britain and America that R. A. Davenport, in his introduction to the 1825 reprint, wrote; "As a translator, he had the field almost entirely to himself; there being at that time no English translation of the Mohammedan civil and spiritual code, except a bad copy of the despicable one by Du Ryer. His performance was universally and justly approved of, still remains in repute, and is not likely to be superseded by any other of the kind."[5]

Sir Edward Denison Ross, in his introductory note to the 1877 edition, echoed Davenport's praise, as he wrote, "when it first appeared, it had no rival in the field; it may be fairly claimed today that it has been superseded by no subsequent translations."[6]

But a quick fact check reveals an obvious thing. The currently available version on the Project Gutenberg contains the notation 'Translated into English from the Original Arabic'. But that is definitely not true as Davenport wrote: "On what authority this is asserted it would now be fruitless to endeavor to ascertain. But that the assertion is an erroneous one, there can be no reason to doubt; it being opposed by the stubborn evidence of dates and facts".[7] George Sale had no knowledge of Arabic. He translated it from the Latin translation of Maracci, as has been noted by Abdullah Yusuf Ali and many other sources. As a member of the Society for the Promoting of Christian Knowledge, he was actually preparing a tool for the conversion of Muslims to Christianity.

---

is Prefixed the Life of Mahomet, ... with a **Needful Caveat**, or Admonition, for Those Who Desire to Know What Use May Be Made of, or If There Be Danger in Reading, the Alcoran (1649).

[5] **George Sale:** The Koran: Commonly Called the Alkoran of Mohammed. Translated into English from the Original Arabic, with explanatory notes taken from the most approved commentators. To which is prefixed a preliminary discourse by George Sale. The Project Gutenberg of the Koran. A Sketch of the Life of George Sale by R. A. Davenport.

[6] Ibid, INTRODUCTION by Sir Edward Denison Ross

[7] Ibid, Sketch by R. A. Davenport.

Following the method of Bishop Kidder for the conversion of Jews, he prescribed four rules for the conversion of Muslims. He held a firm conviction that Christianity was the only true religion. In his note TO THE READER[8] he made that very clear by asserting: "They must have a mean opinion of the Christian religion, or be but ill grounded therein, who can apprehend any danger from so manifest a forgery:" as the Qur'an. He was advocating that the Christians, who professed the only 'True Religion', did not need to have any fear from Islam because its Prophet was an 'Imposter' who taught a 'false religion'. But he also had something positive to say about the Prophet of Islam "for how criminal soever Mohammed may have been in imposing a false religion on mankind, the praises due to his real virtues ought not to be denied him". Even though he had contempt for Islam and its Prophet, he was, at the same time impressed by the success of the Muslim Empire and the spread of Islam which, unlike Alexander Ross who declared that it was accomplished by the sword, George Sale praised as the strength of the system. "I shall not here inquire into the reasons why the law of Mohammed has met with so unexampled a reception in the world (for they are greatly deceived who imagine it to have been propagated by the sword alone), or by what means it came to be embraced by nations which never felt the force of the Mohammedan arms, and even by those which stripped the Arabians of their conquests, and put an end to the sovereignty and very being of their Khalifs: yet it seems as if there was something more than what is vulgarly imagined in a religion which has made so surprising a progress."[9] It was such praise for the success of Islam and Muslims for which he was condemned by many of his own people, who accused him of elevating Islam to the 'high level' of Christianity and even called him a secret Muslim.

George Sale's translation and commentary was re-printed in 1764 and a copy was acquired by Thomas Jefferson. That copy is in the Library of Congress now and was used by Congressman Keith Ellison to take his oath of office when he was elected to the Congress.

Next English translation was by John Medows Rodwell, an English clergyman, in 1861.

---

[8] Ibid, TO THE READER by George Sale
[9] Ibid, TO THE READER by George Sale

**Translations by Muslims**

This has led Muslim writers to venture into the field of English translation.

Abdullah Yusuf Ali pointed that the "amount of mischief done by these versions of non-Muslim and anti-Muslim writers has led Muslim writers to venture into the field of English translation."[10] He noted the English translation of Dr. Muhammad 'Abdul Hakim Khan, of Patiala, published in 1905, that of Mirza Hairat of Delhi published in Delhi in 1919 and Nawwab 'Imad-ul-Mulk Saiyid Husain Bilgrami of Hyderabad, Deccan, who translated a portion, but did not live to complete his work.

The Ahmadiya Sect's Qadiyan Anjuman published a version of the first Sipara in 1915. Its Lahore Anjuman published Maulvi Muhammad 'Ali's translation in 1917. He also noted Hafiz Gulam Sarwar's translation published in 1930 or 1929, and Mr. Marmaduke Pickthall's translation published in 1930. Abdullah Yusuf Ali lamented that Mr. Pickthall "has added very few notes to elucidate the Text. His rendering is 'almost literal': it can hardly be expected that it can give an adequate idea of a Book which (in his own words) can be described as 'that inimitable symphony the very sounds of which move men to tears and ecstasy.' Perhaps the attempt to catch something of that symphony in another language is impossible. Greatly daring, I have made that attempt. We do not blame an artist who tries to catch in his picture something of the glorious light of a spring landscape."[11]

During the nineteenth century, English became a widely used language because the British Empire had expanded far and wide. By the early part of the twentieth century, English had become a world language and there was need for English translation of the Qur'an. The earlier English translations by Alexander Ross and George Sale were neither adequate nor very accurate.

English translation of Maulana Muhammad Ali (1875-1951) was published in 1917. Muhammad Marmaduke Pickthall (1875-1936) published his translation in 1930. Muslims have been attached to many Arabic words which they use routinely in writing or speaking in any language, regardless of the reader's or listener's faith or ability or inability to understand these

---

[10] Abdullah Yusuf Ali, Tranlation of The Quran, page xvi.

[11] Ibid, page xvi.

words. One would find that some Jews display the same tendency to use Hebrew words in conversations while speaking in English. Muslims are particularly insistent on using the Arabic word Allah for God, even though there may not be any need for it. Farsi word for God is Khuda but in religious writings even the Iranians, writing in Farsi or any other language, prefer to use Allah. Indians use both Allah and *Khuda* in common conversations and writings but in religious writings their preference is also for Allah. Maulana Muhammad Ali was an Indian; he used Allah in his English translation rather than the English word God. Marmaduke Pickthall was an Englishman who was born a Christian; he became Muslim in 1917, the same year in which the translation of Maulana Muhammad Ali was first published. Pickthall completed and published his translation in 1930. He stated that his was the first English translation of the Qur'an by a Muslim Englishman for the English. At the first incidence of the name of God, in Chapter 1, he commented in the footnote that he did not consider God to be an adequate translation for Allah and therefore he planned to use Allah in the rest of the Book. That is what he did.

## Abdullah Yusuf Ali – His Purpose

The next Muslim to publish an English translation of the Qur'an was Abdullah Yusuf Ali. He was also an Indian. Born in Bombay in a wealthy merchant family, Abdullah Yusuf Ali (1872-1953) spent a major part of his intellectual pursuit in Lahore. The Subcontinental tradition is for a child to learn to read the words of Qur'an at a very early age. Since many of the languages spoken by the Subcontinental Muslims use the Arabic script, children can learn, and are taught, to read the Qur'an without the ability to know the meanings of what they are reading, because they do not know and are not taught the Arabic language. It would be like an English-speaking child being able to read the words of Spanish without knowing what they mean. When a child completes the first reading of the entire Qur'an, the family celebrates it with a big party. It is like the Bar Mitzvah ceremony for a Jewish boy but at a much younger age, anywhere from 5 years to 10 years, whenever the child finishes the first reading. "It was between the ages of four and five that I first learned to read its Arabic words, to revel in its rhythm and music, and wonder at its meaning"[12] Abdullah Yusuf Ali tells us in the Preface to the first printing of his translation of the Qur'an. He had

---

[12] Abdullah Yusuf Ali, Preface to First Edition, 1934, page iii.

learned to read the words of the Arabic Qur'an but could only 'wonder at its meaning' because he did not know Arabic. He later learned Arabic, first from his father and then from other sources. In school he learned English. He also memorized the Qur'an, and he could recite the entire Qur'an from memory. That is another cherished Muslim tradition; parents of a child who can memorize the Qur'an are very proud. By the time he began his comprehensive study of the Qur'an, began to translate it into English, and undertook the task of writing a very detailed commentary, Abdullah Yusuf Ali had acquired an incredible command on both Arabic and English. And he knew other languages too.

Abdullah Yusuf Ali approached the task of translating the Qur'an with a mission, and dedicated his life to it. That journey took him 40 years and finally culminated in 1934 with the publication of his wonderfully accurate translation and highly comprehensive commentary; **The Holy Qur'an: Text, Translation and Commentary.** His command of the two languages shines through his work. He did not avoid calling it The Qur'an as Pickthal had done by calling his translation 'The Meanings of the Glorious Qur'an' and Maulana Muhammad Ali had referred to his work as 'English Translation of The Holy Qur'an'.

"The service of the Qur'an has been the pride and privilege of many Muslims. I felt that with such life-experience as has fallen to my lot; my service to the Qur'an should be to present it in fitting garb in English. That ambition I have cherished in my mind for more than forty years."[13] With that determination, Abdullah Yusuf Ali dedicated his life to the study of the Qur'an with a mission, which he explains in his Preface to the 1934 printing. "I have collected books and materials for it. I have visited places, undertaken journeys, taken notes, sought the society of men, and tried to explore their thoughts and hearts, in order to equip myself for the task. Sometimes I have considered it too stupendous for me, – the double task of understanding the original, and reproducing its nobility, its beauty, its poetry, its grandeur, and its sweet practical reasonable application to everyday experience. Then I have blamed myself for lack of courage, – the spiritual courage of men who dared all in the Cause which was so dear to them."[14]

---

[13] Ibid, page iii.
[14] Ibid, page iii-iv.

His dedication was not only to learn to understand the finer intricacies and meanings of Arabic, the source, and English, the destination, so he could comprehensively grasp the meaning and express them lucidly for his intended English reader. It was also to familiarize self with the subject matter on a personal level. For that purpose, he travelled extensively to all the places that Qur'an may be understood to mention or even allude to. He studied archeological records and visited archeological sites to learn about the people, ancient or contemporary, mentioned in the Qur'an. He studied the scriptures and other writings of the world religions and made a scholarly comparison with the contents of the Qur'an. He studied literatures in multiple languages and drew on what he read heavily in his Commentary on the Qur'an. He intended for his work "to give to the English reader, scholar as well as general reader, a fairly complete but concise view of what I understand to be the meaning of the Text"[15].

Abdullah Yusuf Ali praises with admiration the high quality of voluminous work generated in earlier times from the study of the Qur'an on which "so much talent, so much labor, [and] so much time and money have been expended". But he laments that "the quality of the later literature on the subject leaves much to be desired". The causes of the decline in this quality are well known. "With the retrogression of the Islamic nations in original work in science, art, and philosophy, and the concomitant limitation in their outlook and experience in various phases of intellectual and spiritual life, has come a certain limitation in the free spirit of research and enquiry. The new Renaissance of Islam, which is just beginning, will, it is hoped, sweep away cobwebs and let in the full light of reason and understanding."[16] His work was a big step in that direction; to expand the outlook and shine the light of reason and understanding. He appeared to express a desire to avoid "theological controversies or enter into polemical arguments" and to concentrate on "more important matters on which present-day readers desire information. In this respect our Commentators have not always been discreet."[17]

---

[15] Ibid,1934, page v.

[16] Abdullah Yusuf Ali, Commentaries on The Qur'an, page ix.

[17] Ibid, page v.

**Qur'anic Exegesis – Commentaries on the Qur'an**

Tafsir literally means 'explanation', but it has come to almost exclusively mean 'explanation of the Qur'an'. It refers to the exegesis of the Qur'an and thus the interpretation of the Qur'an is known as Tafsir in Arabic. In the course of an extensive effort in the science of Tafsir by scholars, other scientific disciplines were developed, such as Kalam, formal logic, *Ilm-ul-'Aqāid*, the philosophical exposition of the grounds of our belief, and *Taawil*, esoteric exposition of the hidden or inner meanings.

Sufi mystics played an important role in the development of these sciences. But while the Sufi mystics remained true to the strict discipline of their Order, "many of the non-Sufi writers on Taawil indulged in an amount of license in interpretation which has rightly called forth a protest on the part of the more sober 'Ulama. For my part I agree with this protest".[18]

Abdullah Yusuf Ali agreed with that protest as he himself stated. He declared that, while each writer has the right of individual judgment, in making interpretation he "must stick as closely as possible to the text which it seeks to interpret". He should use all his knowledge and experience in his analysis but "he must not mix up his own theories and conclusions, however reasonable, with the interpretation of the Text itself".[19] An interpreter's tendency to influence his interpretation with his own personal judgment and belief would be a problem because it has the potential to draw conclusions at variance with the intended lesson of the source, or perhaps even opposite to that intention.

The problem goes beyond the personal judgment and belief of the interpreter; it may derive from his understanding of the language and words he is reading. Arabic, like any other language, has not remained static over the last millennium and half; it has undergone a double transformation over time. On the one hand it has grown and progressed through the natural process with the passage of time, like any other language. On the other hand, being the language of Islam and as such of special importance to Muslims all over the world, many of its words have, over time, acquired special meanings which tend to obscure their actual meanings as intended by the Qur'an and understood by the Prophet and early Muslims. "Arabic words in the Text have acquired other meanings than those which were

---

[18] Ibid, page x.
[19] Ibid, page x.

understood by the Apostle and his Companions. All living languages undergo such transformations. The early Commentators and Philologists went into these matters with a very comprehensive grasp, and we must accept their conclusions. Where they are not unanimous, we must use our judgment and historic sense in adopting the interpretation of that authority which appeals to us most. We must not devise new verbal meanings."[20]

But that is what we have done; we have devised new verbal meanings for many of the words. This has led to variations in people's understanding of Islamic principles causing a movement of the thinking of the faithful towards literalism. "God's purpose is eternal, and His plan is perfect, but man's intelligence is limited at its very best."[21] When that limited intelligence is burdened with the complexities of a changing language and man's personal beliefs which may have been influenced by not only the changed language itself, but also the cultural environment in which the man lives, it becomes necessary to be careful in accepting the pronouncements of that man. One individual may experience fluctuations in the level of his intelligence according to the variations in his powers and experiences. Humanity, collectively, would multiply those fluctuations immensely, from age to age and from people to people. "There is thus no finality in human interpretation. And in the thing interpreted – God's Creation – there is constant flux and change."[22] The view of the same object from various angles would be different when that object is in a static position. But if the object itself is moving, there is a double cause of variation in the view. "So, I believe in progressive interpretation, in the need for understanding and explaining spiritual matters from different angles. The difficulties that confront me may not be the same as those that confront you. The problems which our age has to meet may not be the same as the problems which puzzled earnest minds of the fourth or sixth or later centuries of the Hijra. Therefore, it is no merit to hug the solutions offered in the fourth or sixth centuries when our souls cry out in hunger for solace in the fourteenth century of the Hijra."[23] Abdullah Yusuf Ali wrote this almost a hundred years ago. We are now in the fifteenth century of the Hijra.

---

[20] Ibid, page x.
[21] Ibid, page xi.
[22] Abdullah Yusuf Ali, Commentaries on The Qur'an, page xi.
[23] Ibid, page xi.

In making a distinction between the knowledge based on reports of what happened or was said in the past or how things were done at that time, and knowledge based on judgment and wisdom gained from those reports to determine how it bears on our lives today and either benefits or harms us, it is necessary to opt for the latter. "It is not only our right but our duty to seek honestly our own solutions, and while we respect authority, we must not neglect or despise the gifts which God has accumulated for us through the ages."[24] World has changed and the humanity has made tremendous strides in learning and understanding their environment. We are better equipped to know our needs and our problems. Our enhanced knowledge should enable us to gain a better understanding of the Quranic teachings and to employ God's guidance in solving our problems and in advancing our station on this earth. "In the application of spiritual truths to our own times and our own lives, we must use every kind of knowledge, science, and experience which we possess, but we must not obtrude irrelevant matter into our discussions."[25] When advanced knowledge provides detailed explanation of natural phenomena which humans have always known from observation, there is no need to question the technical details which everyone may not be able to fully understand. "When we speak of the endless plains of India, we are not put on our defense because the earth is round. Nor will such poetic expressions as the seven firmaments raise questions as to the nature of space in modern astronomy. Man's intellect is given to him to investigate the nature of the physical world around him. He forms different conceptions of it at different times. Spiritual truths are quite independent of the question, which of these conceptions are true. They deal with matters which are beyond the ken of physical science. In explaining or illustrating them we shall use such language as is current among the people to whom we speak."[26]

With strong commitment to 'use such language as is current among the people to whom we speak' Abdullah Yusuf Ali proceeded to prepare an English translation of the Qur'an in which he used words only of English. Departing from the earlier Muslim translators, he did not retain a single Arabic word in his English translation. Where the previous two had retained

---

[24] Ibid, page xi.
[25] Ibid, page xii.
[26] Ibid, page xii.

Allah as the name of God, Abdullah Yusuf Ali used the English word God throughout.

The British Empire at this time was in its full strength. It used to be said that sun never sets on the British Empire to indicate its vastness. English language had become, or was on its way to become, a world language. This fact, combined with his mastery of English language, created the need for an English translation of the Qur'an and made Abdullah Yusuf Ali the right person to do it. "In choosing an English word for an Arabic word a translator necessarily exercises his own judgment and may be unconsciously expressing a point of view, but that is inevitable."[27]

He was the best qualified person to select the best English words to express the ideas of the Arabic words in the Qur'an, because of his excellent knowledge of both languages. He was a great admirer of the English language and wanted "to make English itself an Islamic language"[28]. In making this translation, his desire was that the 'rhythm, music, and exalted tone of the original should be reflected in the English Interpretation'. He succeeded in that desire, but it created at least one small drawback. His translation is a great source for many, but hard to understand for the masses. If someone is willing to read the translation, then go on to read the notes for a better understanding, and go further to consult, for a fuller understanding, the references he has so generously and graciously provided in abundance, that someone would be pleased with the great benefit received. But only a few can do all of that.

In addition to the style, his selection of English words also offers a great advantage and a slight problem at the same time. True to his desire to find the best expression in English, he has gone deep into the language to find words which definitely provide the best expression but some of them are so uncommon that they are unfamiliar to most readers and therefore very difficult to understand. For that reason, his work is very popular with those with some measure of scholarly knowledge but not with the great masses who do not possess as much knowledge.

## Fruits of a Forty (40) Year Dedication

Abdullah Yusuf Ali undertook this project during the first half of the twentieth century, finishing it in 1934 and completing it by 1938. He

---

[27] Abdullah Yusuf Ali, Preface to First Edition, 1934, page v.
[28] Ibid, page iv.

strongly advocated in the Preface to First Edition, 1934, and in Commentaries on the Qur'an, to avoid theological controversies and polemical arguments and to concentrate on 'more important matters on which present-day readers desire information'. He expressed hope that the new Renaissance of Islam would 'sweep away cobwebs and let in the full light of reason and understanding'.

He favored 'progressive interpretation' where the interpreter would refrain from devising 'new verbal meanings' and from mixing up 'his own theories and conclusions, however reasonable, with the interpretation of the Text itself'. But it must be a testimony to the prevailing environment of the time and the literalistic tendencies of his contemporary Muslims that this bold and courageous scholar par-excellence felt the need to hedge. "It will be found that every verse revealed for a particular occasion has also a general meaning. The particular occasion and the particular people concerned have passed away, but the general meaning and its application remain true for all time. What we are concerned about now, in the fourteenth century of Hijra, is: what guidance can we draw for ourselves from the message of God?"[29]

Publication of **"The Holy Qur'an: Text, Translation and Commentary"** began in 1934 and was completed by 1938. It soon became widely accepted and has remained a highly respected English translation and commentary to-date. It was published in a single volume by McGregor & Werner, Inc. in the USA in 1946. All quotes from Abdullah Yusuf Ali in this chapter are from that edition, a copy of which is in the possession of this writer. The original publication included the Arabic Text, English Translation, Commentary and a number of explanatory comments and introductions by Abdullah Yusuf Ali to explain the contents and how to read them, along with a comprehensive index.

Later, when the need for the English Translation alone was felt, it was printed and distributed also. There might be two reasons for printing the English only editions, a practical one and a sentimental one. The practical reason was to make it available to all, many of whom only could, or only wanted to, read the English and may not be able to read the Arabic text and may not want to be burdened with extra writings. The sentimental reason was not that obvious but was equally important. Muslims generally feel that

---

[29] Ibid, page v.

Qur'an is really the Arabic Text and, it being sacred, should be handled with respect. Since it cannot be guaranteed that everyone would handle it with the requisite respect, it would be better not to make the Arabic text available to everybody. Anyone who desires to read its meaning should be afforded access to it in the language they can read. Qur'an is by now available in just about every language of the world.

## Saudi Revision – Purpose and Method

Saudi Government desired to make the message of the Qur'an available to those who lacked the knowledge of Arabic. But they also had some concerns. "Given the depth as well as the sublimity of the Qur'anic text, a faithful translation of it into another language is virtually impossible. The various translations that exist today, however accurate they may be, cannot be designated as the Qur'an, since they can never hope to imitate the diction or the style of the Book of Allah. But as translation is one of the few ways to export the message of the Qur'an to allow those lacking in knowledge of Arabic to share this priceless gift, it becomes a duty for those in a position to fulfil this task"[30]. This effort began with an observation which, perhaps, was the foundation of the Saudi effort: "Before the reader begins to study the Qur'an, he must realize that unlike all other writings, this is a unique book with a supreme author, an eternal message and a universal relevance."[31]

Saudi Editors were aware of the various existing English translations of the Qur'an, but they considered all of them inadequate and erroneous. "A

---

[30] **Saudi Revised Edition:** The Holy Qur'an; English translation of the meanings and Commentary: Revised & Edited by The Presidency of Islamic Researches, Ifta, Call, and Guidance, P. O. Box 3561 Al-Madinah Al-Munawarah: 1413 AH, page v-vi.

[31] Ibid, page iii. This statement would appeal only to such who believe in the message of the Book. Any who do not believe in the message would find it neither sacred nor eternal nor relevant. The same sentiment is expressed by all believers about the sacred scriptures of their faith; Jews would say the same about Torah and Tanach or Talmud, Christians would say the same thing about Gospels and the other books of the New Testament, and Hindus would say the same thing about Gita and the other sacred books of their faith. Just as the Muslims would not accord the same level of sacredness and sanctity to the sacred books of other faiths as do the respective believers of those other faiths, Muslims should not be surprised to find that others may not hold Qur'an as sacred and eternal and relevant as the Muslims do. But that is where the problem lies. Every believing people adopt a narrow view to look inward only. Each group not only holds their own sacred books to be exclusively and universally sacred, eternal and relevant but also demand that everyone else should also accept them as such.

number of individuals have in the past ventured to translate the Qur'an, but their works have generally been private attempts, greatly influenced by their own prejudices".[32] They felt the need for a translation that would be free from prejudices of the translators and would receive an official sanction from so high an authority as the Saudi King. "In order to produce a reliable translation free from personal bias, a Royal decree (No. 19888, dated 16/8/1400 AH) was issued by the Custodian of the Two Holy Mosques, King Fahd ibn Abdul Aziz, at the time the deputy prime minister, authorizing the General Presidency of the Department of Islamic Researches, Ifta, Call and Guidance to undertake the responsibility of revising and correcting a particular translation which would be selected for this purpose and made publicly available later".[33] That date corresponds to 30 June 1980. For this purpose, committees of well-qualified scholars were appointed. "The first committee was given the task of examining the existing translations and choosing the most suitable among them. The committee discovered that there was no translation free from defects and so there were two options open for consideration: the first was to select the best translation available and to then adopt it as a base for further work as well as a source of reference, with the objective of revising its contents and correcting any faults in view of the objections raised against it; the second was to prepare a fresh and independent translation, starting from scratch".[34] After some study it became obvious to the committee that "the second option demanded much time and effort, neither of which was available at the time".[35] The committee decided to follow the first option, as a practical matter. "The translation by the late Ustadh ABDULLAH YUSUF ALI was consequently chosen for its distinguishing characteristics, such as a highly elegant style, a choice of the words close to the meaning of the original text, accompanied by scholarly notes and commentaries."[36]

As the committee began to 'revise' and 'correct' **The Holy Qur'an, Text, Translation and Commentary by Abdullah Yusuf Ali**, it stated that it "was fully aware of all the criticism that had been directed against this translation and which had been carefully brought to the notice of the

[32] Ibid, page vi.
[33] Ibid, page vi.
[34] Ibid, page vi.
[35] Ibid, page vi.
[36] Ibid, page vi.

presidency by a number of academic bodies and other involved parties".[37] It was not explained exactly what that criticism was. The completed work was "referred to a number of individuals and organizations who then augmented any deficiencies in the work of the committee".[38] After the completed work was examined and re-examined by a number of bodies and individuals on multiple levels, the committee "arrived at a text as authentic and defect-free as was humanly possible".[39]

It was not explained as to what standard was used to decide that it was 'as authentic and defect-free as humanly possible'.

It was also realized that there were "some Arabic words which could not be translated correctly".[40] They were retained in transliteration and explained in the notes. A list of all such words was also appended. That list begins with Allah and contains 15 more words.

"Finally, a fourth committee was formed to look into the findings of the second and third committees and to implement the recommendations made by them. Furthermore, this committee had to finalize the text by adopting the most accurate expression where needed, besides checking the notes vigilantly so as to clear any misconceptions regarding the articles of faith, varying juristic opinions and thoughts not in conformity with the sound Islamic point of view".[41]

Thus, it would appear that the effort which was claimed to be undertaken to achieve a product – free from personal bias – was really aimed at promoting the orthodoxy according to the Saudi concept of Islam.

Another Royal decree was issued on 16 July 1985. "According to the Royal decree (No. 12412 dated 27/10/1405 AH), this translation is printed at King Fahd Holy Qur'an Printing Complex in Al-Madinah Al-*Munawarah* and also with coordination of the General Presidency of the Department of Islamic Research, Ifta Call and Guidance."[42] It was directed to be distributed to all Muslims and those seeking spiritual light among English-speaking people. The Saudi Edition acknowledged in the Preface, as quoted above, that it was the translation and commentary of Abdullah Yusuf Ali

---

[37] Ibid, page vi-vii.
[38] Ibid, page vii.
[39] Ibid, page vii.
[40] Ibid, page vii.
[41] Ibid, page vii.
[42] Ibid, page vii.

from which this edition was produced, but his name was not mentioned anywhere else. The edition was published as THE HOLY QUR'AN, English translation of the meaning and Commentary, Revised & Edited by THE PRESIDENCY OF ISLAMIC RESEARCH, IFTA CALL AND GUIDANCE. This writer has a copy of the Saudi edition printed in 1413 AH which corresponds to 1992 or 1993 AD, depending on the month of 1413 AH in which it was printed. That edition does not mention the month or date. The cover page inscribes the location of publication as The Custodian of Two Holy Mosques King Fahd Complex for The Printing of The Holy Qur'an, P.O. Box 3561 Al-Madinah Al-Munawarah. The date of the original publication can be assumed as the date of the Royal decree, July 16, 1985 (27 Shawwal 1405) or soon thereafter in late 1985 or early 1986.

Abdullah Yusuf Ali had explained his mission and work in eight different explanatory notes including prefaces and comments. All of them were excluded from this edition except TRANSLITERATION OF ARABIC WORDS AND NAMES and a somewhat revised version of ABBREVIATIONS USED. However, one finds that the comments retain the personal reference of Abdullah Yusuf Ali, some of which begin with 'I have used . . .' or similar personal notes. Such personal notes are odd to be found in the work claimed to be produced by a committee, or perhaps by a number of committees, as many as four. Such personal references are found in the Transliteration section and in a large number of other comments.

**Saudi Edition Became Worldwide**

The Saudi edition remained the only one available for some time but then many other publishers began to publish it also. These other publishers slowly began to place the name of Abdullah Yusuf Ali on the cover to credit him for the translation and commentary and began to include some or all of his original introductory notes and comments. But his original translation and commentary have not been restored; every current edition printed anywhere in the world, under the name of Abdullah Yusuf Ali, contains the translation and commentary as revised by the Saudi Editors.

There is a report that someone somewhere in the USA has now begun to print the original.

**Saudi Revision – Extent and Impact**

Saudi Editors wanted to "produce a reliable translation free from personal bias" because, as they stated, they had examined the existing translations by a 'number of individuals' and declared that they were 'greatly influenced by their own prejudices'. Saudi Editors desired 'a translation that would be free from prejudices of the translators' because among the currently available ones "there was no translation free from defects". They did not elaborate as to what prejudices of the individual translators they were talking about or what defects they had found in those translations. They selected the work of Abdullah Yusuf Ali to 'revise' and 'correct' about which the committee 'was fully aware of all the criticism that had been directed against this translation'. Here again they failed to specify the criticism that was directed. After about five years of effort, the Saudi Editors completed their work and declared it to be 'as authentic and defect-free as was humanly possible'.

Was it 'as defect-free as humanly possible'? What defects did the Saudi Editors find and rectify in the work of Abdullah Yusuf Ali which they 'revised' and 'corrected'? What errors were in that work which required to be 'corrected'? Was the final publication by the Saudi Editors really free from personal bias?

These questions are hard to answer. And, in a way, even these questions might be seen as biased. Saudi Editors saw personal bias and defects in the existing translations, even in that of Abdullah Yusuf Ali, which they selected for their revision because they found it to be the least biased and the least defective, but biased and defective, nevertheless.

Abdullah Yusuf Ali, following his declared goal of using only English words in his translation, had used the English word God for the name of the Supreme Being. There is a practical reason for it. When one addresses an audience in the language of the audience, one must stay within that language to communicate the intended information. If one includes words of another language which are not familiar to the audience, one creates a situation in which the audience would assume that the speaker or writer is talking about something entirely different. When a Muslim addressing an audience of another faith, such as Christianity or Judaism, in another language, such as English, keeps referring as Allah to what the audience knows as God, he is creating an opportunity for the audience to assume that Muslims do not believe in God, but believe in some other Divine Entity known as Allah. In America one often hears people saying that Muslims do not believe in God; they believe in Allah, who is their own God. Abdullah Yusuf Ali was aiming to overcome that confusion by strictly following the universal message of the Qur'an which repeatedly emphasizes that its message is for all humanity and for all the worlds. By overcoming the linguistic variations, he was trying to bring understanding and harmony to the world, which is the core message of the Qur'an.

The Saudi Editors, who complained about the personal bias of other translators did exactly what they declared they wanted to eliminate; they introduced their own bias by insisting to use the Arabic word Allah as the name of the Supreme Being rather than the English word God in their English translation. By doing that, they confused their English reading audience and differentiated Islam from the faith of their audience, which is just the opposite of the goal of the Qur'an, the Message of God. By that implication they created an impression in the minds of the English readers of the Qur'an who belonged to another faith that Allah is different from God and is exclusively the Deity of the Muslims. At the same time, they impressed upon the Muslims that there is something wrong in referring to the Supreme Being by any word other than Allah, regardless of what language one might be speaking. They found this word in 3,222 places in the Qur'an, in all of which Abdullah Yusuf Ali had written the English word God. Saudi Editors replaced God with Allah in all of those 3,222 places. In addition, they replaced God with Allah in 7,143 places in the commentary and elsewhere; they 'corrected' them all. That was the biggest 'error' the Saudi Editors accused Abdullah Yusuf Ali of, and 'corrected' it all 10,365 times.

**God 10,365 total = 3,222 in text + 7,143 in notes and elsewhere
All changed to Allah**

The Saudi Editors also found the word 'Apostle' as translation for Rasul unacceptable. They changed it to either Messenger or Prophet. It was found 248 times in the translation and 540 times in commentary and elsewhere. They 'corrected' all 788 by changing to either Messenger or Prophet.

**Apostle 788 total = 248 in text + 540 in notes and elsewhere
All changed to Messenger or Prophet**

Abdullah Yusuf Ali had made a promise to his readers that in his translation the 'English shall be, not a mere substitution of one word for another, but the best expression I can give to the fullest meaning which I can understand from the Arabic Text'. With his almost perfect knowledge of both English and Arabic, and 40 years of effort, he did come up with words that in his opinion were the 'best expression' of what he was trying to translate. Apostle comes from Greek apostolos or apostellein; apo- + stellein which means 'to send'. Apostle is similar to messenger, but apostle is a whole lot more comprehensive in meanings than messenger. Abdullah Yusuf Ali selected it to translate the Arabic word Rasul which means a messenger in common usage, but Qur'an uses it in two ways; to designate God's Messengers such as Moses and Muhammad, and also in its common meaning. Wherever it was used for God's Messengers, Abdullah Yusuf Ali translated as Apostle, and in common usage he translated it as messenger. But the Saudi Editors did not like this word perhaps because of its association with the 12 Apostles of Jesus. They found this word 248 times in the Translation and 540 times in the Commentary and elsewhere. They 'corrected' it in all 788 places by changing Apostle to either Messenger or Prophet. This was the second biggest 'error' they considered Abdullah Yusuf Ali to have made. But in fact, they were expressing their own prejudice, and once again they violated their own goal to eliminate bias.

Beyond changing God to Allah and changing Apostle to either Messenger or Prophet, Saudi Editors did not change much. Qur'an is divided into 114 chapters of various lengths. Chapters 103, 108, and 110 contain 3 verses each and are the smallest in number of verses. Chapter 2 is the longest with 286 verses. Total number of verses in Qur'an is 6,259. Thus, there are 114 chapters in the Qur'an containing 6,259 verses.

Saudi Editors made only 14 changes in 14 verses contained in 3 chapters.

None of these changes can be designated as corrections because they all involve replacement of words with other words of similar meaning selected to convey a particular point of view. Saudi Editors had complained about other translators' personal prejudices, declared that those translations had defects, and had stated that they were 'fully aware of all the criticism that had been directed' against the translation of Abdullah Yusuf Ali. But they found very little to change, and whatever they changed was not 'corrections', but an attempt to promote the orthodoxy according to the Saudi doctrine. Abdullah Yusuf Ali had actually attempted to keep his translation free of any attempt to promote a particular point of view and had succeeded in keeping it free of any personal bias. Saudi Editors reversed that in order to promote their own version of the faith.

These 14 changes were made in 14 verses contained in three chapters only – chapters 2, 3 and 14. Abdullah Yusuf Ali uses words such as mystic, metaphor, allegory and their derivatives and refers to Sufi mysticism occasionally. He also likes to refer to people chosen and/or guided by God as 'man of God' or 'men of God'. Saudi Editors displayed a disliking for such words and expressions. Wherever they were found, the Saudi Editors changed them to words of their own liking. These changes show a tendency for the desire to achieve a literal meaning of the Text and narrow it down to a particular point of view. That was exactly what Abdullah Yusuf Ali had declared that he wanted to avoid. He wanted to seek wider meanings in the Text. Majority of the 14 changes made by the Saudi Editors are changes in words or phrases apparently to achieve more literal sense, which was against their own declared goal of a translation 'free from personal bias.'

**The following are from Chapter 2.**

1.  In chapter 2, verse 31, as part of the story of the creation and the education of Adam, God taught Adam *Al-Asma'a Kullaha*. Then God told Adam to tell the angels *Asma'a-e-him*. *Asma'a* is plural of the word Ism which means name. The first phrase literally translates 'the names of all things'; the second phrase translates as 'their names'. God had ordered Adam to display his knowledge of things he had been taught. So, Abdullah Yusuf Ali translated it as 'the nature of all things' and 'their nature' respectively. Saudi Editors considered it to be an 'error' and 'corrected' it to 'the names of all things' and 'their names'. Abdullah Yusuf Ali was reaching out for the substance of the message. Saudi Editors opted for literalism.

2.  In chapter 2, verse 33, repeats the same words as in 2:31 above.

3.  In 2:85 the word is *Udwan*. It could mean enmity, rebellion, disobedience or some other hostility. Abdullah Yusuf Ali translated it as 'rancor'. Saudi Editors 'corrected' it to 'transgression'. Both words have the same meanings.

4.  In 2:114 the phrase 'in places for the worship of God' is followed by a phrase in which God is not explicitly mentioned but is implied. Abdullah Yusuf Ali translated Asmuhu as 'God's name', perhaps for

clarity and emphasis, but the Saudi Editors 'corrected' it to the literal translation 'His name'.

5.  In 2:115, the phrase is *Waj-hullah*, literally meaning 'face of God'. The verse declares that God is everywhere, east or west or wherever one turns. Abdullah Yusuf Ali translated it as the 'Presence of God' in every place and space. Saudi Editors 'corrected' it to 'Allah's countenance'. They should have capitalized that word – countenance – as Presence was capitalized in the original, but they did not.

6.  In 2:132, the context is the legacy of Abraham for his sons and grandsons and the word being translated is *Muslimun*. Abdullah Yusuf Ali translates it as Abraham telling his children to remain in 'the Faith of Islam'. Saudi Editors 'corrected' it so that Abraham was telling his children to remain 'in the state of submission' to God. Whatever reason the Saudi Editors had for making this change, I personally like this version much better. To my thinking they made an improvement here. An improvement is not necessarily a correction.

7.  In 2:151, the phrase being translated is yu-*zakkikum*. Abdullah Yusuf Ali translated it as 'sanctifying you'. Saudi Editors 'corrected' it to 'purifying you'. Both say the same thing.

8.  In 2:165 the word 'a'zab occurs twice. Abdullah Yusuf Ali translated as 'Penalty' both times. Saudi Editors 'corrected' it to 'Punishment' in both places. Again, both mean the same thing.

9.  In 2:221 the subject is marriage, and the commandment is against marriage between believers and non-believers. Abdullah Yusuf Ali translated the word al-*mushrikat* as 'unbelieving women' and parenthetically added (idolaters), perhaps for clarification because the Arabic is really the feminine version of polytheists. Saudi Editors 'corrected' it by removing the parenthetical addition but retained the translation as 'unbelieving women' perhaps in order to widen the scope of the commandment. However, they added a new note, 245-A. Literally "pagan".

**The following are from Chapter 3.**

10. The numbering system of the verses in the Qur'an is almost universal but not 100%. The number of variations is so small, compared to the total number of verses – 6,259 – that it is hardly noticed and seldom

discussed. Abdullah Yusuf Ali pointed out that the "system of numbering the verses has not been uniform in previous translations." He goes on to say that this "is not a vital matter, but it causes confusion in references. It is important that at least in Islamic countries one system of numbering should be adopted. I have adopted mainly that of the Egyptian edition published under the authority of the King of Egypt." He noted and praised an effort on this matter that was under way at the same time. "I am glad to see that the text shortly to be published by the Anjuman-i-Himayat-i-Islam of Lahore is following the same system of numbering. I recommend to other publishers in India the same good example."[43] Thus, Abdullah Yusuf Ali did make an appeal for a universally accepted single system of numbering. The first difficulty he faced was when he reached the beginning of the third chapter. The break between verses 3 and 4 differs in various schools. He had to pick one break. He made his choice and explained it in Note 344. Saudi Editors changed the arrangement by going to a different break. They retained the first part of the Note and deleted the second part. But the part of the Note that the Saudi Editors retained says that the break would be where Abdullah Yusuf Ali made it. Saudi Edition has the break in a different point. Therefore, in the Saudi Edition, the arrangement of verses 3 and 4 does not agree with the Note. This is not a correction; it would rather add confusion.

11. Verse 3:7 confirms the impression that Saudi Editors did not like certain words. This verse contains a profound statement about the contents of the Qur'an. In it, God has declared that the clear statements in the Qur'an are the foundation of the Book, but it also contains statements whose meanings are known only to God and may become understandable to humans in the future when knowledge attains an advanced level. The words of interest here are *mutashabihaat, tashabaha,* and *tawilihi,* which Abdullah Yusuf Ali translates as allegories and hidden meanings. It occurs three times in the same verse and Saudi Editors 'corrected' it as follows: Allegorical changed to 'not of well-established meaning' (*mutashabihaat*); Allegorical changed to 'not of well-established meaning' (*tashabaha*);

---

[43] Abdullah Yusuf Ali, Preface to First Edition, 1934, pages iv-v.

Hidden meanings changed to 'true meaning' (*tawilihi*). These changes may state the meanings in different, and perhaps more common, words, but they do not qualify as corrections by any means.

12. In 3:173, the reference is perhaps to the battle of Uhud in which the Muslims suffered a setback. The focus of this verse appears to be on the dedicated Muslims who remained steadfast in the face of the danger. When they were warned about a great army that was gathering against them in order to frighten them, they became even more determined and more steadfast. Here the same phrase *fakhshauhum* is rendered to the same impact with a slightly different approach. Literally it might be rendered as 'then fear them'. Abdullah Yusuf Ali went for the impact of the phrase by taking it out of the quotation marks and translating its effect as 'and frightened them' meaning those who were warning about the great army tried to frighten them. Saudi Editors took the literal approach and kept it in the quotation marks by continuing the warning in rendering 'so fear them'. Both say the same thing.

13. In 3:184, *zubur* is a word on the meaning of which Abdullah Yusuf Ali has stated that the Commentators are not in agreement. The common belief is that it refers to the Book of Psalms. He translated it as 'books of dark prophesies' and explained his reasoning in Note 490. Saudi Editors understandably took the safe route and translated it simply as 'the Scripture'. Both achieve the desired goal.

14. The only other change made in the Translation by the Saudi Editors is in chapter 14 verse 45. The last sentence was translated by Abdullah Yusuf Ali as: 'We put forth (many) Parables in your behoof'. Saudi Editors changed 'behoof' to 'behalf' which is a more common word and easy to understand by most readers. Once again it points to the kind of command Abdullah Yusuf Ali had over the English language. In fact, behoof is a legitimate word, a noun same as behalf, and means 'that which benefits; advantage; use; and comes from the Old English behof meaning advantage'. True to his mission of finding the most appropriate expression, behoof fits better than behalf. His mission would have been just as nicely accomplished if he had used the more common word 'behalf'. But he was determined to provide the greatest benefit of his knowledge to his reader. In line with that determination, he has used so many words in this work

which most of us mere mortals are unable to recognize or understand. On further review, they all turn out to be not only legitimate but also the best expression for the intended purpose. However, not many of us have time or ability for further review. Saudi Editors opted for simpler words, sometime merely to simplify but sometime also to redirect the reader to their particular point of view.

## Conclusion

Abdullah Yusuf Ali was trying to make the message of Qur'an accessible to the English-speaking people of any and all faiths, in their own language. Saudis turned it into an exercise in proselytization. Their proselytization may or may not have had an impact on their desired readers, those belonging to faiths other than Islam, but it definitely impacted a sizeable majority of Muslims all over the world, especially in countries where Saudi influence pervades. A large number of Muslims were indoctrinated into believing that Muslims should use only Arabic words in theological matters. They became adamant that the Supreme Being should be referred to by no word other than the Arabic word Allah, no matter what language the conversation is in. Pakistanis abandoned the Farsi word *Khuda*, which had been in common use for hundreds of years, openly declaring it to be the wrong word to be applied to God. And of course, the English word God is considered to be even more wrong, as implied by the Saudis in refusing to use it in their English translation of the Qur'an. Abdullah Yusuf Ali was the first Muslim translator of Qur'an who had used the English word God as translation of the Arabic word Allah because, as he stated, he was preparing a translation of the Qur'an for the English-speaking people and therefore used only English words. That was necessary in order to avoid confusing his English-speaking readers with terms they were not familiar with and were liable to assume that Allah – a word potentially unfamiliar to them – was some other entity different from the One True God of the Universe. That is the point which Qur'an drives with extreme emphasis that there is only One True God. He must be called by the word that is most familiar to the target audience. Saudi Editors violated that intent of the message of Qur'an.

Saudi Editors produced two results, whether they were intended or not. Both results caused consequences which are not favorable to the image of either Muslims or Islam. First, they indoctrinated Muslims into Saudi orthodoxy, which compelled Muslims to stand apart from people of all other faiths with an air of superiority in direct violation of the teachings of the Qur'an. This was bound to lead to unnecessary confrontation and conflict. Second, they caused the original work of Abdullah Yusuf Ali, in which he had invested forty years of his life, to disappear into oblivion. Wide publications of the Saudi edited version under the name of Abdullah Yusuf Ali since the late 1980's has created a false impression that it is what Abdullah Yusuf Ali did. Using that scholar's name on the cover of the Saudi version of the translation and commentary, the Saudi orthodoxy was thus validated, causing it to be widely propagated. That is not only unfair to Abdullah Yusuf Ali, but it is also dishonest.

Saudis claimed that they were desirous of an English translation of the Qur'an which would be "free from personal bias". But then they proceeded to transform the translation and commentary by Abdullah Yusuf Ali – which was free from personal bias – and introduced their own personal bias by making an attempt to promote orthodoxy according to the Saudi thought. Abdullah Yusuf Ali had discussed this very point in his preface to the first edition. He stated: "In translating the Text I have aired no views of my own but followed the received Commentators. Where they differ among themselves, I have had to choose what appeared to me to be the most reasonable opinion from all points of view. Where it is a question merely of words, I have not considered the question important enough to discuss in the Notes, but where it is a question of substance, I hope adequate explanations will be found in the Notes. Where I have departed from the literal translation in order to express the spirit of the original better in English, I have explained the literal meaning in the Notes." He conceded an unintended consequence of a translator's effort. "In choosing an English word for an Arabic word a translator necessarily exercises his own judgment and may be unconsciously expressing a point of view, but that is inevitable."[44] Having conceded that point, he went on to advocate caution in a number of areas, a caution which he himself devotedly followed.

First: "To discuss theological controversies or enter into polemical arguments I have considered outside my scope. Such discussions and arguments may be necessary and valuable, but they should find a place in separate treatises, if only out of respect to the Holy Book. Besides, such

---

[44] Abdullah Yusuf Ali, Preface to First Edition, 1934, page v.

discussions leave no room for more important matters on which present-day readers desire information. In this respect our Commentators have not always been discreet."[45]

Second: "While freely reserving the right of individual judgment on the part of every earnest writer, I think the art of interpretation must stick as closely as possible to the text which it seeks to interpret. Every serious writer and thinker have a right to use all the knowledge and experience he possesses in the service of the Qur'an. But he must not mix up his own theories and conclusions, however reasonable, with the interpretation of the Text itself, which is usually perfectly perspicuous, as it claims it to be."[46]

Third: "Arabic words in the Text have acquired other meanings than those which were understood by the Apostle and his Companions. All living languages undergo such transformations. The early Commentators and Philologists went into these matters with a very comprehensive grasp, and we must accept their conclusions. Where they are not unanimous, we must use our judgment and historic sense in adopting the interpretation of that authority which appeals to us most. We must not devise new verbal meanings."[47]

Saudi Editors have not followed these cautions in their work. They have not been discreet in avoiding specific points of view, and in avoiding introducing their own conclusions as to what the message of the Holy Book is or should be. Abdullah Yusuf Ali had undertaken his enormous obligation with the utmost care and caution as he so clearly stated himself. He was creating an English translation of the Qur'an for which he had decided to use only the English words for very good and obvious reasons. Rather than simply replacing Arabic words with English words of similar literal meanings, which can potentially be misleading in many cases, he attempted "to express the spirit of the original". To grasp the real meanings and the very spirit of the message, faithful have always inquired into the message beyond the simple meanings of the words. Those who were fortunate to live in the presence of the Holy Prophet frequently approached him to seek better understanding of the revealed verses of the Qur'an, as Abdullah Yusuf Ali has pointed out. "The need for an explanation of the

---

[45] Ibid, page v.
[46] Abdullah Yusuf Ali, Commentaries on The Qur'an, page x.
[47] Ibid, page x.

verses of the Qur'an arose quite early. Even before the whole of the Qur'an was revealed, people used to ask the Apostle all sorts of questions as to the meaning of certain words in the verses revealed, or of their bearing on problems as they arose, or details of certain historical or spiritual matters on which they sought more light. The Apostle's answers were carefully stored in the memory of the Companions (as-hab) and were afterwards written down."[48] More than the "meaning of certain words", it is crucially important to understand "their bearing on problems", because that is the very purpose of the message; to guide us in our mortal life on this earth. Qur'an declares at the very beginning of Surah Baqara; "THIS DIVINE WRIT - let there be no doubt about it - is [meant to be] a guidance for all the God-conscious." (Qur'an 2:2 – Asad Translation) Abdullah Yusuf Ali had translated it as: "This is the Book; in it is guidance sure, without doubt, to those who fear[26] God." The phrase "fear God" is the translation of the Arabic word Taqwa, which Asad translated as "God-conscious". Abdullah Yusuf Ali explained the word Taqwa in Note 26.

> 26. *Taqwa* and the verbs and nouns connected with the root, signify: (1) the fear of God, which, according to the writer of Proverbs (1:7) in the Old Testament, is the beginning of Wisdom; (2) restraint, or guarding one's tongue, hand, and heart from evil; (3) hence righteousness, piety, good conduct. All these ideas are implied; in the translation, only one or other of these ideas can be indicated, according to the context. See also 47:17; and 74:56, n.5808.

Saudi Editors changed God to Allah in the translation and in this Note but left the Note otherwise completely unchanged.

Abdullah Yusuf Ali produced a translation which is as un-biased as humanly possible. Saudis, on the other hand have set out to "Correct" Yusuf Ali by DELIBERATELY introducing their own biases. It is not the intent of this article to sit in judgement. It only highlights Saudi liberties with the original version and their consequent impact on Muslim Thought and on the relations of Muslims with people of other faiths. The most unfortunate consequence of their unnecessary "correction" is the wide acceptance of this Saudi version as the work of Abdullah Yusuf Ali. Saudi Role in creating that perception may not be clear, and they may not admit it, but it is obvious that this perception is created by Saudi revision of the work of Abdullah Yusuf Ali, and subsequent publication of Saudi version under

---

[48] Ibid, page ix.

the name of Abdullah Yusuf Ali. In the process, the real work of Abdullah Yusuf Ali disappeared and has been forgotten. That served the Saudi purpose because they had declared that they had been "fully aware of all the criticism that had been directed against this translation and which had been carefully brought to the notice of the presidency by a number of academic bodies and other involved parties". It was not explained exactly what that criticism was, and exactly who the critics were, but this statement clearly demonstrates Saudi bias against and displeasure with the work of Abdullah Yusuf Ali in spite of the fact that they did not actually find anything wrong with his translation except for changing 14 words in 14 of the 6,259 verses of the Qur'an into simpler words of the same meaning. The major Saudi complaint was against the use of an English word in English translation for the name of God; Saudi Editors insisted on retaining the Arabic word Allah no matter how much it confused the English reader with no familiarity with Arabic or Islam.

*****

# 10.  Understanding Social Change: Institution of Marriage

*The dominant segment of the population can exercise its control on the institutions of the government and the society, and thus redistribute power, privilege, and wealth. Such powers must, however, be constrained to protect fundamental human rights and freedoms and be non-discriminatory as to various characteristics such as race, skin color, religion, gender, sexual orientation. A case in point is the definition of marriage and the need or lack of need for a marriage license.*

A New York Times Editorial (February 26, 2016) urged the Governor of South Dakota to veto a bill passed by that state's legislature. The purpose of the bill, according to its sponsors, was to "protect the innocence of children." The New York Times called that argument absurd, and argued, with some justification, that there were "good reasons to veto it". However, this episode was part of a much bigger issue that continues to cause a huge emotional debate but has not been handled rationally. It is a problem that demands a solution, but in finding a solution for it, many other problems have been created.

History records human behavior and human activities throughout human existence. Great thinkers have attempted to define the ideal human behavior. Their noble sounding ideas – justice, peace, equality, life, liberty, pursuit of happiness, etc. – generally find wide admiration and praise. But the observed human behavior shows little evidence that humans actually practice any of those ideals; recorded human behavior has always been at odds with all of them.

Humans keep on singing the praises of peace and justice but fail to cite a single moment at any time in human history when either peace or justice prevailed on the earth. Human life appears to be governed by self-interest and self-gratification bordering on greed. While proclaiming to believe in egalitarianism and declaring that "all men are created equal", powerful humans are known to have held countless men — and women and children — as slaves who could be bought and sold as property. It is often considered to be perfectly acceptable as a legal principle to declare and hold certain humans to be not 'equal' but merely as three-fifth of a human. Those created equal must be of a different, but special, kind. "All" are not included in that equality.

To want to dominate others is a basic human instinct. Humans are obsessed with the desire to be superior to others, or at least someone else. Most people strongly hold the conviction that they know they were superior to others. This intrinsic human desire for domination and superiority manifests in a concerted effort to exercise control over the lives of any who are weak enough to be subdued; to take from them the things of value, not only to benefit self but also to deprive them so they would become weak and easy to subjugate. Human history is full of tales of conquests and defeats, empire building and bondage, the occupiers and the occupied. It is a natural outcome of the desire to dominate and the presumption of superiority.

Some people find that they can overpower and control others, so they do it. As Glaucon said to Socrates, justice is the advantage of the stronger. And, as Zod said to Superman, why should ones with advantage give up their advantage. The strong will always exercise their advantage to control and oppress the weak. It is Us versus Them. Us are strong, therefore always right. Them are weak, therefore always wrong. Humans are always dividing themselves into groups of Us and groups of Others. Humans differentiate these groups by characteristics they like and do not like. Our characteristics are likable because they are familiar to us; we are comfortable with them. Anything different is always wrong and must be condemned. We have familiar habits and customs; these are right. Everything else is wrong and must be declared as an abomination.

The strong impose their will on the weak. That happens all the time. The strong subdue the weak and demand that they abandon everything that defines them — their identity and their values — and adopt the values of the dominant. If any resist, they face dire consequences. Values create the difference and only the values of the strong are allowed to survive. These 'superior' values are sacred and are sanctified. Their superiority is proclaimed based on race, religion, gender, sexual orientation and nationality of the dominant. It is imposed by their power.

Even in a democracy, where leaders acquire positions of power by the consent of the people through elections, those who come to people to seek their consent become the absolute controllers of the people's lives after they move into the position and begin to exercise the power given to them by the people. Those who place such leaders in power often suffer from the excesses of its exercise.

Change is anathema to human sensibility. Change is opposed, resisted and condemned. Every new religion, every new movement, every new idea has always been fiercely opposed at first. Change has often led to wars, destruction, oppression, and genocide. Those favoring and adopting the change are always the victims at first, until they themselves can rise to become dominant. Then they proceed to victimize those whom they can subdue.

Human race is characterized by patriarchy practicing a system of male domination. Misogyny has always been practiced. There was time when misogyny was so rampant that men hated to father a female child. Every father wanted a son. In some areas, they used to even kill their newborn daughters. Misogyny may have subsided somewhat in modern times, but it has not completely disappeared. World remains a patriarchic and male dominated society. In some parts of the world, men are using the ultrasonic technology to determine the gender of an unborn child. If it is female, they force the mother to have an abortion. Even in societies where such practices do not happen, women are not afforded proper respect. Even if a few may have broken the glass ceiling to create an illusion of progress, society in general continues to practice misogyny in a more sophisticated fashion.

Heterosexuality has been held as the gold standard throughout human history. But it is obviously not the only sexual orientation displayed or expressed by humans. Even Bible acknowledged an alternate by implication without speaking about it directly. There is no express judgment or condemnation of Homosexuality in the Bible except Lot's use of the word 'wicked'. That brief implied mention in three verses of Genesis has been the basis of religious condemnation of homosexuality, holding it as an abomination. Civilized nations with advanced legal systems used to have laws on their books which prescribed capital punishment for "the detestable and abominable vice" of homosexuality.

"The Meek shall inherit the earth" leads to the hope that everyone can expect to have their day in the sun by finally being able to come out of the closet. Humanity has always known about the existence of the homosexual orientation which human society adamantly rejected, condemned and severely punished. Even after the scientific research theorized that it is caused by a complex interplay of genetic, hormonal, and environmental influences, and is a natural outcome rather than a choice, human society refused to reduce its hatred. However, in the second half of the twentieth century, things began to change a little. Stonewall rebellion of 1969 in New York City is generally held as the starting point of gay civil rights movement. A 2003 ruling by the U.S. Supreme Court effectively decriminalized homosexual relations nationwide. Another ruling by the U.S. Supreme Court in 2015 legalized same-sex marriage in all fifty states.

The Supreme Court recognized their humanity and their civil rights, but opposition remained, from the religious authority and many other powerful circles. State legislatures began to introduce laws in the name of Religious Freedom to limit the civil rights of those belonging to LGBT community. Indiana passed such a law in 2015 which was signed by Governor Pence. Mississippi and South Dakota followed. The New York Times editorial was about South Dakota legislation. Many more states are pursuing such bills, all in the name of Religious Freedom.

Supreme Court recognized the humanity and the civil rights of the LGBT+ community. Some people support that decision, but a large number are opposed. While many people continue to consider the whole idea to be an abomination, one element is particularly aggravating for them; the word 'marriage' used for the same sex union. It is unnecessary and can be avoided.

Problem solving technique, taught in school, begins with an analytical understanding of the problem, proceeds to finding different possible solutions, assessing each of these solutions, and arriving at the selection of the best possible solution to the problem at hand. That technique may be used in the science lab or a professor/scholar's study, but it is not used in real life to solve everyday problems. Rational behavior may be essential to deal with the puzzles of life, but rational behavior rarely finds its application in human attempts to overcome the difficulties which humanity faces on a daily basis. Human decisions are hardly ever rational; they are almost always emotional.

Take for example the current new life-style issue of same-sex relations. A rational look at this problem presents it as an issue of civil rights, human rights, economic and financial opportunity, and a social issue of dignity and acceptance. But the whole debate on this situation is emotional with hardly any rational thought devoted to it. Those opposed to this phenomenon approach the issue from their lifelong indoctrination of the whole idea as being an 'abomination'. They consider those who claim this lifestyle and demand a right to practice it as 'sinners' and therefore subject to rejection from society and exclusion from the human race. They consider such people to be corrupt human beings; they desire to sentence them to doom.

These opponents forget that people they are condemning are in fact human and, under the prevailing human laws and accepted norms of human and civil rights, they are entitled to the same inalienable rights which other human beings possess and freely exercise. Their demand for equal treatment under the laws of the land, without prejudice and discrimination, is fully justified. They must be afforded the opportunity to avail themselves of the same benefits and privileges under equal protections of the laws governing tax code, employment and housing, and all other areas of citizenship.

While they have fully legitimate rights to be treated as equal, they are also presenting their demands with an emotional approach rather than a rational one. Perhaps the emotional approach is more powerful in achieving objectives, but it leads to undesirable consequences. It generates opposition rather than cooperation. The effort turns into a struggle and becomes combative. It may achieve a measure of success if it succeeds in persuading some powerful elements to render their support. But the opposition would continue to simmer and may one day explode, especially if the opposition also succeeds in persuading powerful elements to render their support in the reverse.

Equal protection of the law is the right of all humans regardless of the various differences, all of which are now protected under the existing laws. LGBT community has the right to be afforded the same protection under the law and must be treated with dignity and respect as human beings, free from prejudice and fear of danger of any kind, as long as they obey the law and the other norms of the society like everyone else. Same sex unions must be afforded all the benefits and protections of the tax code, inheritance and family support and relationship. But it must be recognized that the same sex union is not exactly the same as heterosexual marriage. Reproduction is the one huge difference between the two. If some people object to the use of the word 'marriage' for same sex union, they have a point, and their sensitivities need to be respected. If one phenomenon is not exactly the same as another, there is nothing wrong in using a different word for it. But that is the rational approach which is not too popular when an emotional approach is so palatable and provides so much power.

The situation is further complicated and made confrontational by an irrelevant and unnecessary requirement of the need to obtain a permit to get married. So many people openly complain about the government being too involved in their lives and loudly demand to get the government off their backs. But nobody has ever complained as to why people are required to obtain a permit to get married. A boy and a girl, or if you prefer a man and a woman, are totally free to decide by themselves who to marry. And nobody, including their parents, has any right to interfere. It is their life and only they have the exclusive right to make that decision, who to marry and when and where to get married. Then why should they be required to obtain the permission of the government? The government can claim the right to keep records of marriages and the marital status of individuals. That can be done by filing something after the marriage has taken place without the need to obtain permission to get married. Births and deaths are recoded after the fact. Nobody is required to obtain permission to be born or give birth, or to die. Marriages can similarly be recorded after the event. That would remove one source of battle for the same sex union, whatever we decide to call it.

Marriage license is a system of control exercised by the government in times when it was felt necessary, and was possible, to ensure that the 'right' people do not marry the 'wrong' people. In such times the distinction between the 'right' people and the 'wrong' people was obvious and clear. It was known to all and held sacred by the 'right' people who held it to be their inalienable right to preserve the purity of the 'right' people. Since the 'right' people were in complete control of all the institutions of power, they were fully capable of enforcing the rules of preservation. The requirement to obtain the permission of the government to get married by applying for a marriage license ensured that the purity of the 'right' people would be preserved because any attempt at a violation would be discovered and quickly quashed.

Times have changed and the distinction between the 'right' people and the 'wrong' people appears to have disappeared, at least on the surface. Political correctness has made it inappropriate to speak of that distinction regardless of how strongly such distinction may be held in unspoken secret thoughts. The requirement for marriage license has lost its purpose but the practice continues because it has become a habit that nobody has thought of changing or getting rid of. People have been so accustomed to obtaining a license to get married that it has become sort of a part of the nature of the society which is blindly followed without giving any thought to its need or usefulness or even wonder if it may cause any harm.

The same sex phenomenon has shone the light on the uselessness of the practice and on the harm it can cause. Supreme Court declared that same sex union is legal, but those with authority to issue marriage license have frequently denied the license. The need to screen who can marry whom, having disappeared or at least been rendered impossible to achieve, it is time to do away with the requirement to obtain a marriage license to get married. If the bride and groom are free to choose each other without interference from anyone, even their parents, then they should be free of the need to obtain the permission from the government to get married. After the fact, they can be required to register with the government for the purpose of official record keeping so that they are able to claim privileges confined under the law to married couples only. Anyone who does not care for those privileges should be free not to register if they choose not to.

When Supreme Court legalized the same sex union as marriage throughout the land, the Justices neglected to address the issue of the requirement of marriage license. Protection of the human and civil rights of every segment of the population is a duty of not only the Supreme Court but also of all the branches of the government. While protecting the rights of one segment, the rights of the other segments of the population must not be ignored; everyone's rights need to be protected. There should not be a tradeoff to grant rights to one segment by denying or suppressing the rights of others. All citizens have equal claim to the free exercise of their legitimate and lawful beliefs and customs. Those with the power to decide who can enjoy what rights have an obligation to adopt a fair and balanced approach. The rights of same sex union must be acknowledged, granted and protected, but their exercise must not be allowed to subjugate the rights, practices and sensibilities of anyone else. In solving one problem, care must be taken to avoid creating other problems. It is not appropriate to let the legal system follow the tradition of prescription medicines where just about every prescribed medicine almost always generates unintended but harmful side effects. Doctors mostly shrug these side effects off by telling the patients to grin and bear them. The legal system and the Supreme Court would do better by not adopting this attitude of the medical and pharmaceutical professions. The marriage certificate requirement has to be terminated. Those wanting to get married should be able to do so any time and any place of their choice without facing any obstacle from the government authority. They can be required to register their marriage after the fact in a government office or by mail. The required forms should be easily available, including online, and online registration should also be an option.

Those assigned the responsibility to protect the rights of all citizens – all branches of the government, especially justice and law enforcement – have a sacred obligation to diligently provide those protections to all citizens in accordance with the laws of the land. As the need becomes evident, the legislature must develop and enact new laws to address these needs. However, it must be recognized that while protection can be legislated and enforced, compliance with the intended protections can also be enforced. But the requirement for all people to associate and establish friendships with all others can neither be legislated nor enforced. Everyone can be forced to refrain from interfering with the other's free and secure exercise of their rights under the law, but nobody can be forced to associate and make friends with everyone else, or to willingly and happily participate in everyone else's activities. All people, individually and collectively, have the right to form associations and friendships with whomever they please. They can do it selectively because associations and friendship are by their very nature selective based on what people like. With some exceptions, even business and professional associations cannot be legislated nor enforced. Any attempt to do that would violate the same rights of those being compelled as the ones being granted to others. Only a totalitarian government would attempt to do that. A representative government of the people, for the people, by the people should be committed to defend and protect all, to afford everyone to live in accordance with their beliefs as long as they do not violate the law of the land and do not deny others their rights or          interfere          with          their          exercise.

# 11. *Rattled by Cultural Wars: Emergence of Trumpism*

*This chapter is based on an article written in November 2016, following the election of Donald Trump as the US president.[1] Emergence of Trumpism in 2016 was not an abrupt event that just happened, rather, it was a continuation from what was happening in the American society since long. It reflected change in the attitudes of people as their fortunes changed, their livelihood tightened, their politicians wavered, and their religious leaders emboldened.*

On the election day for the 2016 presidential elections, I served as an election judge. After a very long and tiring day, I came home dead tired and went to sleep. I woke up at 3 am and made the mistake of turning the TV on. Then I could not sleep. I have not felt normal ever since.

I do not listen to the news, do not read the news, and do not want to know what is happening in the political arena. I used to watch comedic talk shows and used to enjoy their political satire. I do not watch them anymore, because I no longer find them funny.

The comedic value in their content was based on their suggestion about what would happen if certain situations materialized, with the implication that those situations can never materialize because they are not normal for human behavior. But now, all those situations have materialized. Therefore, such political satire is not funny anymore; it is now actually painful.

I feel something but I do not rightfully know what. It could be fear, it could be anger, it could be indifference, or it could be any combination of all of those and many other emotions. I do feel some kind of numbness, a

---

[1] This article was published in Arab Daily News. It is available at this Link. http://thearabdailynews.com/2017/01/12/election-results-paralyzed/

certain amount of mental paralysis, and definitely a diminished capacity to think and act.

I feel kind of lost. There is an extreme degree of uncertainty which fogs the view into the future. It is hard to see what is coming.

I have been in America since 1964 and an American citizen since 1979. I have seen the American society, and its attitudes and thinking, go through many transformations. I witnessed the birth and growth of the political correctness. The ideal manifestation of political correctness was civility; for people to be careful in their public discourse by choosing words which would not be offensive to others. The movement was designed to develop respect for, and sensitivity to, cultural, ethnic, racial and religious diversity. Its hope was that the people over time would become not only sensitive to, but also respectful of diversity, thereby creating harmony among people of various different backgrounds.

It must have worked for some people but apparently did not work for all. For many people, the practical manifestation of the political correctness was to shield their inner feelings during their public discourse. They may have never changed their inner feelings and thoughts about the 'other', the people who were different from them. But it taught them not to let their inner thoughts become part of their public discourse. They built a barrier between their true feelings about others and their public interaction with those others. The political correctness became such a powerful force that some people were compelled to create that barrier to hide their true feelings.

Two things happened over the last few years which finally broke that barrier.

First, it was weakened by the economic downturn which began in 2007 and became really painful for a large number of people very soon. The economy has improved since then, but while that improvement is highly visible in aggregate numbers, the fruits of its improvement are not widely distributed. There are still a whole lot of people who continue to feel the hurt; they hurt badly.

Second, it was weakened by an unprecedented level of foreclosures, high unemployment whose visible aggregate improvement hides the serious underemployment and dwindling earnings, the rising cost-of-living greatly outpacing the earnings and thereby squeezing a large number of people hard pressed to make ends meet, and the general lack of recognition of these conditions by the power structure which continues to applaud the economic recovery without paying ample attention to its lack of distribution and lack of availability to a large number of people feeling the pinch of the economic squeeze. Those hurt badly from these conditions were angry at their governmental leaders' lack of proper attention to their plight. Their anger was intensified by their growing sense that their leaders did not care about them.

These conditions and situations had begun to weaken the barrier between the inner feelings and outer expressions created by political correctness. Then, an openly vicious election campaign finally cracked that barrier wide open. The statements which had become taboo over the last 50 years were now openly shouted by some of the political candidates. People who were hurting and were angry, found those shouts to be an open invitation to throw away the political correctness barrier and openly express their true inner feelings.

The dream of a united American nation created by a harmonious multiculturalism was over. The road was open for a badly divided nation.

The elements of division began to manifest during the very night following the Election Day and have continued. Churches, Synagogues and Mosques have continued to be vandalized, with the vandals leaving hateful statements on buildings and signs. Individuals and groups are being harassed on the street, in the buses and trains, in the workplace or market area, in the schools, and in other public places.

The election has not yet been consummated and all these things are already happening. What should be expected or feared after the new power structure takes over?

Perplexed in such a situation one seeks a solution, a way out, an escape. I started thinking and searching. I was badly in need of something to lean on because I was unable to stand, feeling weak and lost, completely unsure of what to do. I started reading to comfort myself.

I found something in the words of Muhammad Iqbal, the great poet-philosopher of India. What he said was not comforting as much as it was an explanation of what I was going through, what we are all going through. "Why are you puzzled by your wandering in the desert?" Iqbal asks; "Don't you know that the unending struggle is the very evidence of Life?" Iqbal insists that this constant struggle is an integral part of life. He even calls it the very essence of life, the evidence that we are living.

That made me recall something that a wise sage once told me; that the test of faith is in the way we react to difficulty and adversity. If our faith is strong, we consider adversity to be a test, which we must endure and strive to pass. But if our faith is weak, then we consider the adversity to be a punishment from God, and we complain like crazy but fail to resolve it. My faith must be very weak because I always consider any difficulty to be a punishment. I do not want to be tested. I hate being tested.

Am I unique in this respect? I hope not. If there are others like me, I have a request for them. Let us stop complaining and get to work to take and pass the test. Let us listen to what Gandalf told Frodo in the Mines of Moria. Frustrated by the never-ending misery, Frodo cried; "I wish the Ring had never come to me and none of this had happened". To which Gandalf replied, "So do all who live to see such times. That is not for them to decide. All they have to decide is what to do with the time that is given to them".[2]

It is times such as the ones we are facing now which compel us to consider and even accept the concept of predestination, no matter how much logic may argue against such a thing. In the words of Omar Khayyam; "The Moving Finger writes; and, having writ, moves on: nor all thy Piety nor Wit Shall lure it back to cancel half a Line, Nor all thy Tears wash out a Word of it." So, it is no use to be witty or even to shed tears. It is time to do something to improve our lot.

If we are destined to play the hand that is dealt to us, and struggle through whatever life throws at us, we need a plan to make the best of it. Iqbal provides some guidance for that also. "Oh you, who are eager to die for the Truth, first create some life in your lifeless body of clay." Life is necessary for a body to function. To say something, one has to be living; a body has to have a life. A lifeless body cannot produce sound. Lifeless body has no sound.

Many years ago, a prominent and successful Democratic Leader explained to a small group of us the difference between Democratic Party and Republican Party. He said that the Democrats always had hard time deciding what they want or do not want, and they just keep on intellectualizing. The Republicans always know exactly what they want, and they go straight for it without any hesitation.

---

[2] The Lord of the Rings, Part I. The Fellowship of the Ring, Tolkien.

How true! This election has illustrated this point so clearly. The Democrats could not decide who to support or who to oppose. Then a large number of them became so entangled in their own indecisiveness that they just could not leave home on the Election Day, handing the election over by default. How do they feel now? Are they proud of their indecisiveness?

Can we hope to have learned the lesson and have decided to overcome our self-inflicted malaise? Can we hope to become decisive and agree to focus? To paraphrase Iqbal, "Salvation lies in cooperation, coordination and unity of purpose, but unfortunately my people are as yet ignorant of this principle".

Those of our Leaders, who are at least pointing out the right way, need to cooperate, coordinate and unite for the common purpose. They need to recognize the sufferings of millions who have not yet been able to recover from the economic downturn of a decade ago and reach out to them with solutions, real solutions and not just meaningless talk. American people are very decent people, and they are fully capable of recognizing the real effort at making the improvement. They are also very smart; they can recognize lack of effort and indifference. This election has shown this. Real change is now needed.

# 12. The Current Political Environment and the Way Forward for American Muslims

*I belong to three communities. My main community is the American Nation of which I am a proud member as a US citizen. I also belong to two subsections of the great American Nation; the American Muslims and the Pakistani Americans.*

*This chapter is addressed to my two communities, the American Muslims and the Pakistani Americans.*

*The new trends in the US society and political environment with respect to the minorities and the requirements for political correctness, underscore how the Muslim community is ill prepared to cope with the challenges. It needs to heed the changing winds, get united for the challenge, and start platforms and actions to protect their rights, and the rights of the future generations. They would need to draw on their cultural heritage to energize the community, such as on the philosophy of Allama Iqbal and the message of Quran.*

The New York Times of 28 June 2018 discussed the possible consequences of the retirement and replacement of Justice Anthony Kennedy. It declared: "In the simplest terms, the Supreme Court is likely to begin siding more often with those who already have power – and against those who don't have much." That prophetic statement turned out to be so accurate. Supreme Court continues to play an activist role with harmful consequences for a large number of helpless people. It was a profound statement with far reaching consequences for the American Muslim Community. Already, some of us have observed that "In the current political and social environment of USA the American Muslim Community

149

does not receive human respect, citizen's dignity, equal justice, and proper image depiction." In view of the current composition of the US Supreme Court, this predicament of Muslims in USA continues to become direr.

Already, some of us have observed that "In the current political and social environment of USA the American Muslim Community does not receive human respect, citizen's dignity, equal justice, and proper image depiction."[1] In view of the current composition of the US Supreme Court, this predicament of Muslims in USA is likely to continue to become direr.

Ray Hanania of the Daily Arab News (7/17/2018) declared; "Left doesn't care about Muslims, only uses them as wedge". Then he went on to explain: "Activists on the Left often claim that they champion the rights of others including Muslims and sometimes Arabs, but the truth is they really don't support us. They just don't mind using us for their own political agendas. Activists on the Left have been no less critical of Muslims and Arabs than activists on the Right. A recent controversy created by the Huffington Post involving Congresswoman Debbie Dingell and gubernatorial candidate Abdul El-Sayed is a good example." The whole article is in this link[2], and it is well worth the time anyone invests in reading it.

I have been thinking about this situation since the US Presidential election of 2016. That election had serious consequences for the American Muslims. We all remember the Muslim ban and similar other policies which targeted the American Muslims in particular and Muslims in general.

I began to ponder the plight of American Muslims and how could the situation be improved. I found some guidance in the words of the great poet philosopher Mohammad Iqbal. It was quoted in the previous chapter that Iqbal had declared that the constant struggle is the evidence of life.

As I kept on reading, I found that so many people have said the same thing to reinforce the idea of our helplessness in the face of fate from which there is no escape. Life is something we did not ask for, we were not given a choice if we wanted to be born or not, it was simply imposed on us along

---

[1] Prof. Abdur Rahim Choudhary in the Muslim Voice News Journal.
[2] https://thearabdailynews.com/2018/07/17/left-doesnt-care-about-muslims-only-uses-them-as-wedge/?utm_source=feedburner&utm_medium=feed&utm_campaign=Feed%3A+The ArabDailyNews+%28The+Arab+Daily+News%29

with the obligation to live it by rules not of our making nor in our control. That is what was made very clear by Ghalib when he said.

قید حیات و بند غم اصل میں دونوں ایک ہیں
موت سے پہلے آدمی غم سے نجات پائے کیوں

*Life and Sorrow are in fact one and the same:*
*There is no escape from Sorrow before Death.*

Ghalib declares that death is the only portal by the passage through which one may secure freedom from Sorrow. Khawaja Ghulam Farid agrees when he declares.

غلام فریدا ایہ روونا انج مکسی جدوں بنھیاں کفن دیاں تنیاں

*Ghulam Farid, this crying sorrow will end only when one is wrapped in a burial*
*shroud.*

However, Iqbal does not seem to agree with this negative portrayal of life. While agreeing and declaring that life is bound in a constant struggle, he appears to find something positive in that struggle which, he believes, offers endless possibilities of success and great achievement.

پُختہ تر ہے گردشِ پیہم سے جامِ زندگی
ہے یہی اے بے خبر رازِ دوامِ زندگی

*Life is fuller and stronger because of the constant turmoil.*
*This is the very secret, very essence of life's eternal nature.*

He goes on to actually advocate a constant struggle and demands that humans should engage in this endless struggle to create continuous change for the better, to reach higher and higher levels.

جس میں نہ ہو انقلاب موت ہے وہ زندگی

رُوحِ اُمم کی حیات کشمکشِ انقلاب

*Life without a revolutionary change is death.*
*The essence of the history of nations is the constant revolutionary struggle.*

He believes and wants everyone to subscribe to his belief that it is very possible for man, by striving through constant revolutionary struggle, to reach such a high living state where God is so pleased that He grants us our every wish.

خودی کو کر بلند اتنا کہ ہر تقدیر سے پہلے

خدا بندے سے خود پوچھے بتا تیری رضا کیا ہے

*Raise your self-esteem so high that before deciding your fate!*
*God would have to ask you: "What is your wish?"*

So, if we are destined to play the hand that is dealt to us, without any ability to alter or modify it, then we need a plan to make the best of it. Iqbal provides some guidance for that.

ہو صداقت کے لیے جس دل میں مرنے کی تڑپ

پہلے اپنے پیکرِ خاکی میں جاں پیدا کرے

*The heart that beats with a burning readiness to sacrifice itself for the Truth —*
*Should first create a powerful life in his body made from the dust of the ground.*

Life is necessary for a body to function. To say something, one has to be living; a body has to have life. A lifeless body cannot produce sound. Lifeless body has no sound.

The body of American Muslims is lifeless; at most it barely has life. For that matter, so is the body of Pakistani Americans. Millions of individuals, all scattered and busy in their individual pursuits, cannot draw attention to their common plight even if a few of them individually engage in a very strong effort to speak out and reach out. Individual voices are like the stress calls in the wild which are heard by no one. And even if they are heard, they fall on deaf ears. Who would pay attention to a lonely caller who has no backing and might even be expressing a hollow sentiment purely for personal recognition!

People can sense the hollowness and see through the lack of substance.

My grandfather used to tell the story of a dying man who called his 11 sons to his bedside. He gave each of them a stick and asked them to break it. They all broke their sticks with no difficulty at all. Then he took 11 sticks and tied them securely in a bundle.[3] He asked them to break the bundled sticks. They all tried their best, but no one could break them. Anyone reading this is likely to say that they have heard the story before. That is good. So, you know the lesson of the story. We American Muslims and we Pakistani Americans are going around with our individual sticks which carry no strength at all. In fact, most of us do not have any sticks at all; only a few of us do. Those few, each of whom does own a stick, should not attempt to go it alone to solve all the problems of the community single-handedly. Those who are genuinely concerned for the community and are working alone for the benefit of the community will fail to achieve any success unless they learn to work with the community, take the community with them and pool the efforts of many and participation of all. Those who are trying to achieve personal glory may succeed in some instances, but the community will not draw any benefit from their success.

The American Muslim Community, by its devil-may-care attitude, appears to be bent on committing *Atma-hatya*, Hara-kiri. It is indifferent to its own sad situation. Either it is ignorant of its plight or does not care. Most everyone is, as Iqbal declared, **haath pe haath dhray muntzir e**

---

[3] The Old Man and His Sons, also known as The Bundle of Sticks, is an Aesop's Fable. It has been told in different versions.

*farda.* (Sitting on their hands, waiting for tomorrow.) Facing such precarious times and situations, it is high time that we the Muslims in USA follow the advice of Iqbal to stop waiting for tomorrow and make our tomorrow with our own efforts. Quran tells us that we have to strive ourselves before expecting anything from God; وَأَن لَّيْسَ لِلْإِنسَٰنِ إِلَّا مَا سَعَىٰ *"Humans can have nothing except what they strive for"*[4]. There is no free lunch. Those who have a desire to shake the community out of its slumber, need to devise a plan to motivate everyone, or at least most of them or enough of them, to wake up, be energized and become organized. Many attempts have been made but participation is always woefully meager. Changing that is of primary importance.

As a Muslim I reach into the Qur'an and find that God has declared that He is not going to help anyone who does not take the first step to help themselves. Those who make an effort to improve their lot will find the help of God available to them. But we have to take the first step before we can expect God to render any help. Quran declares: إِنَّ اللَّهَ لَا يُغَيِّرُ مَا بِقَوْمٍ حَتَّىٰ يُغَيِّرُوا مَا بِأَنفُسِهِمْ *God will never change the condition of a people until they begin to change it by themselves.*[5]

We are American Muslims. Most of us migrated to this country from various other lands, such as Pakistan, India, Middle East, Far East, Africa and Europe. All of us have settled in America, have become US citizens and have made a good life for ourselves and for our families. Then there are many US born Muslims. While many of us may have done well on an individual level, we have not done all that well as a community. We should now move to that second level and begin to organize to achieve recognition for us as a community and protection for our rights as citizens of this great country.

I have been in America since 1964. During this time, I saw several transformations in American thinking and attitudes. American majority did not treat the minorities well, but the Muslims received a comparatively better treatment and even some respect. Then the political correctness began to take roots and created a significant variant between what the majority thought and felt, and how they expressed it in public. Negative statements about minorities became politically incorrect and therefore

---

[4] Quran 53:39
[5] Quran 13:11

unacceptable in public expressions. But 9/11 brought another transformation. Political correctness continued to hold for all other minorities, but it began to dissipate for Muslims and Islam. About us, the American Society began to bridge the political correctness barrier between inner thoughts and public expressions. They began to openly and publicly express their inner thoughts, which were not very nice. Some minorities were also emboldened to join in that public expression to demonize Muslims and Islam.

It has been rightfully noted that the American Muslim community does not receive respect. Respect is a fundamental human right. But there is another element to the idea of respect; it has to be earned. We cannot sit idle behind closed doors and expect humanity to come knocking at our door for the simple purpose of professing their respect. If we isolate ourselves or decide to stay aloof, we can expect to be ignored. We may even be demonized for being different and aloof. That is happening, and for a good reason.

If they do not know us, they are going to assume things about us. What they assume is not going to be good or pretty; it is going to be bad and ugly. And we are not going to like it; that is for sure. So why not prevent them from assuming by reaching out to them and introducing ourselves so they get to know us, and they do not have to assume.

Late Dr. Aftab Ahmad Khan (1917-2006) was very passionate about how Muslims should inform the world about themselves and their religion. He founded the Islamic History Society and frequently came to Maryland to hold seminars. He used to say that if we do not tell our story, who will? If we let others tell our story, they will not tell the real story, and definitely will not tell the way it should be told. Only we can tell our real story and tell it right. Listen to what others are saying about us and read what they are writing, and we see the wisdom of what Aftab Bhai said.

The prevailing narrative about us is at such a great variance from reality. We have an obligation to correct it and bring it in line with reality. Qur'an makes it an obligation on us to get to know each other; not only introduce ourselves so that the others know us well, but we should make every effort to know them. جَعَلْنَاكُمْ شُعُوبًا وَقَبَائِلَ لِتَعَارَفُوا *We made you into nations and tribes so you may know each other.*[6]

---

[6] Quran 49:13

Lately, our situation has further deteriorated, especially since the presidential election of 2016. Remember the Muslim Ban. It was struck down by just about every court in the land. But it was finally upheld in the Supreme Court. We are just now hoping that it will go away. But will it? What if it is brought before the Supreme Court, which has now been further transformed?

*Let us see how America views us.*

New York City launched a program under Mayor Bloomberg to infiltrate and spy on the Muslim Community. When Bill de Blasio became Mayor in 2014, he announced that the program would be terminated. It was not, at least not at that time. Who knows, it might still be going on. The thinking behind that program was somebody's a Muslim, Muslims are potential terrorists, therefore we investigate Muslims. When questioned by media about civil rights, an official simply brushed it off by saying that the need to prevent terrorist attacks sometimes came into conflict with the need to respect constitutional rights. Under this program, at least one undercover detective of NYPD was exposed to have pretended to "convert" to Islam to spy on Brooklyn College students. When that detective was exposed, Muslim students were understandably angry. One student expressed that anger by saying that to be honest it hurts to think that the surveillance-induced trauma I've had to deal with is simply dismissed as collateral damage. He added that this I am told is for my own good, for public safety – and just like that I find myself outside the scope of who qualifies for that safety.

That is the very basic point. We are frequently excluded from the official concern for safety and protection, and actually targeted as the culprits without any evidence of wrongdoing, simply because we are Muslim.

The program named Countering Violent Extremism (CVE) was established to counter all violent ideologies. But it was applied exclusively to the Muslim Community. Federal officials spoke at Rutgers University about CVE to local police, community groups, and media. The discussion by the law enforcement agencies focused primarily on what they called Islamic extremism. That kind of disproportionate amount of attention focused on our community is unfair and troubling. "If something is caused by a Muslim, it's immediately labeled terrorism but if it's caused by a white supremacist, it is labeled as a lone wolf who is mentally disturbed or has some family problems."

Available data make it absolutely clear that most of the terrorist acts are committed by non-Muslims in the United States, but they are never called terrorist acts. During the three years – from 2018 to 2020 – there were 1,371 mass shootings in which 1,425 persons were killed and 5,975 were injured. Only one incidence was designated as a terrorist act. A Saudi aviation student killed three U.S. Navy sailors and wounded eight on December 6, 2019, in Pensacola, Florida. It was designated as a terrorist attack directed by al-Qaeda. Among the remaining 1,370 incidents, one was actually an anti-Muslim act. It was an attack on a Mosque in California; Mosque was set on fire. Thank God, no one was hurt. But an act of violence instigated by institutional hate for Muslims did not receive the label of terrorism.

When a crime is committed by some misguided Muslim, it is endlessly broadcast on TV and radio, and in print news media. Islam is always declared to be the cause. And the entire Muslim Community is held responsible and is required to collectively apologize. When someone of another faith commits a crime – and that happens so frequently – the media reports it as normal news and no one besides the ones who committed the crime is held accountable. The religion of the shooters is never blamed; it is not even mentioned. The pattern of Anti-Muslim discrimination is so visible and so prevalent that it cannot be missed. But it is routinely denied and brushed off. The Guardian (12/14/2015) reported that the day before Trump announced his Muslim ban, Marco Rubio claimed that Islamophobia is fictitious. He asked: "Where is the widespread evidence that we have a problem in America with discrimination against Muslims?" Their eyes are open, but they cannot see.

Freedom of Speech is guaranteed by the US Constitution. But what does it look like? Who is entitled to it? Rubio must definitely be entitled to it, to state an obvious lie. Many others feel entitled to say things without caring if they bear any resemblance to truth. Here are some examples.

These people hate Muslims, have heard about something called Sharia Law and decided to use their Constitutional right of free speech to come and terrorize Muslims in our places of worship. This happens frequently all over the country and they are allowed to freely terrorize the Muslim worshipers inside our places of worship in the name of "free speech". They, or the authorities allowing them and protecting them in this act, must not have heard about the Constitutional right to freedom of religion. It would seem that the authorities do not care about that freedom of religion for the Muslims; they allow these people to terrorize Muslims like this, and even protect them while they are doing it. If I was inside one of those Mosques surrounded by angry mobs, I would be terrified to death. I can imagine how those worshippers inside these mosques must have felt. But these people have freedom of speech which must be protected as sacred. Remember when Trump told four members of congress to go back where they came from. It was reported all over the media on July 14, 2019. But nobody pushed back.

*So that is the way things are. How do we improve them?*

First let us ask: Do we have freedom of speech? The answer is yes and no. We have it, but it is not as sacred and not as unlimited as theirs. Still, we do have some, very limited, freedom of speech. But the problem is that we are not using even that highly limited freedom of speech. That is the very point which we need to ponder.

Estimates of American Muslim Community are claimed to run up to eight million in America. Montgomery County, Maryland has a large Muslim Community, perhaps 70,000. So many individuals, all scattered and busy in their individual pursuits, cannot draw attention as a community even if a few of them individually engage in a very strong effort to speak out and reach out. It is hard to draw attention to a few lonely voices with no community backing. In Pakistan we used to say that one is one but two standing next to each other is like eleven. Those who speak with the full support of the community would draw attention and be respected.

We often complain that we are not being heard. Someone asked; 'If they are not being heard, whose fault is that?' Could it be that we are not speaking? A few individuals may be active and speaking out, but the vast majority of our community is silent. We need to change that. We need to reach out, to speak up and become visible. A few of us are already doing it. We need to thank them and follow their lead. We can join boards and committees, become members of any political party and become active in the party's activities at any level starting from a precinct. We can seek elective offices and support other candidates. Some of us are already doing that but not really enough. Many more need to step up and participate. Such efforts to participate would be of great benefit to our community. Quran tells us that God rewards us only when we make an effort and also that God does not improve the condition of a people until they themselves make an effort to change it.

Let us proceed to organize our community to gain the proper respect and secure our rights. The British Muslims have done much better. We should learn from them.

Our community members generously contribute to political candidates. Tufail Ahmed (1936-2022) was a long-time prominent leader of our community, our Big Brother. Tufail Bhai always told us that politicians love our community because we contribute but never ask for anything in return. We need to ask because nobody is going to do anything for us on their own.

But, before we ask, we have to know what to ask. We must determine what our needs are, what issues are important to us and what concerns we need to address. We need to develop a platform listing our goals and objectives based on our needs, issues and concerns. The platform must be such that the community can willingly subscribe to it. Therefore, it must be developed with full community participation. A community that accepts and adopts a platform and commits to support only those candidates who agree to honor our platform and make a commitment to support it, becomes a voting bloc. Something like six or eight million Muslims in America and 70,000 in Montgomery County; those are formidable numbers, but only if we are united, only if we fall behind a common purpose, a common platform. If we do not, we will continue to be invisible to the power structure and continue to be neglected. As I mentioned before, one is alone but two become eleven. Alone we are weak, but together we are strong. If we unite under a common banner, we can be a force to reckon with. That is what distinguishes all the successful political organizations. We can be one too, if we are willing to work for it. It will not be easy and will not happen overnight. It would take a long time and a lot of hard work. But it can be done. Muslims did it in UK. We can do it here. When we succeed, we will not need to go to the office seekers. They will come to us and be willing to do our bidding. Then our financial contributions would bring major dividends for our community.

We need to organize ourselves into one cohesive unit which must speak with one voice. We can have all the differences among ourselves within the community, we can internally argue with each other until kingdom comes, but when we go out and interact with others, we have to present a united voice. That is the only way we can expect to receive the attention of the powers structure and accomplish something for the collective good of the community. Iqbal made this point very forcefully. He was commenting about the people around him, not only the Muslims but all the people of Asia, most of whom were in pretty sad state then, and continue to remain in much the same state even today. What he said about the people around him applies equally to us, the American Muslims and the Pakistani Americans. This has been quoted once before and repeated here for emphasis.

ربط و ضبطِ ملّتِ بیضہ ہے مشرق کی نجات
ایشیا والے ہیں اس نکتے سے اب تک بے خبر

*The cohesive organization of the Radiant Community is the salvation of the East.*
*But the people of Asia are so far ignorant of this principle.*

Just as organization was, and remains, the salvation of Iqbal's people, so is organization the salvation of American Muslims and Pakistani Americans. Iqbal was concerned that the Asians were unaware of this need for organization. He would be distressed to know that equally unaware are the Pakistani Americans and American Muslims. He would definitely warn us that نا سمجھو گے تو مٹ جاؤ گے. (If you do not understand your plight, you will be wiped out.) And he would be right.